One Day at a Time in Phobics Victorious

Rosemary

One Day at a Time in Phobics Victorious
Second Edition
Phobics Victorious
Founded 1993
rosemaryjane@dc.rr.com

ISBN 978-0-9972085-5-9 (paperback)
ISBN 978-0-9972085-4-2 (ebook)

Published by AquaZebra, www.AquaZebra.com

AquaZebra™
Book Publishing

Author: Rosemary

Book Designer Mark E. Anderson, AquaZebra

AquaZebra™
Web, Book & Print Design

www.AquaZebra.com

Library of Congress Control Number: 2016942469
Library of Congress - United States Copyright Office
Certificate of Registration
TX 4-248-426

Printed in the United States of America

What is
Phobics Victorious?

Phobics Victorious is a Christ centered recovery program and ministry for people suffering and recovering from irrational fears, phobias, and acute panic attacks.

Phobics Victorious is based on the Twelve Step approach to recovery as used in such fellowships as Alcoholics Anonymous, Narcotics Anonymous, Overcomers and Alcoholics Victorious.

Phobics Victorious is also a tool by which suffering phobics can learn about our Higher Power, Jesus Christ. In Phobics Victorious, we declare Jesus Christ as our Higher Power. In following the Twelve Steps of Phobics Victorious, we are led to a knowledge of Jesus Christ as our Lord and Savior.

Through our desire to learn about Jesus Christ, through our commitment to Him as our Higher Power, and through following Jesus, the Holy Scriptures, and the Biblically based Twelve Steps of Phobics Victorious, we are led into freedom and victory over fear.

Are you a phobic? Ask yourself the following questions to learn if you need help in recovering from fears, phobias, panic attacks, anxiety, and to see if you know Jesus Christ as your personal Savior.

1. Do you ever experience the following symptoms to such an extent that they interfere with your everyday functioning?
   - rapid heartbeat
   - intense fear, panic
   - paralysis of action
   - dread of impending doom
   - embarrassment
   - desire to escape
   - inability to leave your home
   - inability to communicate effectively with others
   - fear of heart attack or going crazy
   - loss of control
   - avoidance of places, people

2. Do you rely on alcohol or drugs to function in phobic situations?

3. Do you worry excessively, catastrophisizing, anticipating the worst?

4. Do you lack faith in God or in yourself?

5. Do you know who you are?

6. Do you want to be free from irrational fears and panic attacks?

We in Phobics Victorious look to Jesus Christ for our recovery. We study the word of God, the Holy Bible, and we follow the Christ-centered Twelve Steps of Phobics Victorious. We fellowship with other suffering, recovering, and freed phobics in Phobics Victorious. We meditate on our daily affirmation book, One Day at a Time in Phobics Victorious.

If you are open-minded, honest and willing, the spiritual journey of the Twelve Steps of Phobics Victorious, with Jesus Christ at the center, will transform your life. One day at a time, as we let go and let God, and surrender our lives to Him, we receive peace, serenity, and freedom. We become new creations in Christ: healthy, whole and free.

Twelve Steps of
Phobics Victorious

1. We admitted we were powerless over the enemy, fear, and that our lives had become unmanageable.

2. We came to believe that a power greater than ourselves, the Lord Jesus Christ, could restore us to sanity.

3. We made a decision to turn our will and our lives over to the care of God the Father, His Son Jesus Christ and His Holy Spirit.

4. We made a searching and fearless moral inventory of ourselves.

5. We admitted to God, ourselves, and to another human being the exact nature of our wrongs.

6. We became ready to have God remove our shortcomings.

7. We humbly asked Him to remove our defects of character.

8. We made a list of all persons we had harmed and became willing to make amends to them all.

9. We made direct amends to such people whenever possible, except when to do so would injure them or others.

10. We continued to do a daily personal inventory and when we were wrong promptly admitted it.

11. We sought through prayer and meditation to improve our conscious contact with God the Father, His Son Jesus Christ, and His Holy Spirit, praying only for knowledge of His will for us and the power to carry it out.

12. Having had a spiritual awakening as the result of these steps, we tried to carry this message to others and to practice these principles in all our affairs.

The Twelve Steps of Alcoholics Anonymous

1. We admitted we were powerless over alcohol — that our lives had become unmanageable.

2. Came to believe that a Powee greater than ourselves could restore us to sanity.

3. Made a decision to turn our will and our lives over to the care of God as we understood Him.

4. Made a searching and fearless moral inventory of ourselves.

5. Admitted to God, to ourselves and to another human being the exact nature of our wrongs.

6. Were entirely ready to have God remove all these defects of character.

7. Humbly asked Him to remove our shortcomings.

8. Made a list of all persons we had harmed, and became willing to make amends to them all.

9. Made direct amends to such people wherever possible, except when to do so would injure them or others.

10. Continued to take personal inventory and when we were wrong promptly admitted it.

11. Sought through prayer and meditation to improve our conscious contact with God, as we understood Him, praying only for knowledge of His will for us and the power to carry that out.

12. Having had a spiritual awakening as the result of these steps, we tried to carry this message to alcoholics, and to practice these principles in all our affairs.

I sought the Lord, and He heard me, and delivered me from all my fears.

Psalm 34:4

As a recovering suffering phobic who has experienced the devastating bondage of acute panic attacks, I will keep my focus on my Higher Power, Jesus Christ. It is through the power and strength of my Higher Power that I am set free. Fear no longer paralyzes me.

Today, I believe that my Higher Power, Jesus, is delivering me from my fears and that I am healthy, whole, and free. I have received liberty. Thank You, Higher Power!

January 2

God is our refuge and strength, a very present help in trouble. Therefore will not we fear.

Psalm 46:1-2

Today I will find strength in my Higher Power. It is not my strength that will see me through the feared situations, but my Higher Power's strength in me.

Regardless of outward circumstances and how fear provoking they can be, I will find refuge in God, for His Spirit is mightier than all physical reactions. His power releases me from fear.

January 3

The fear of man bringeth a snare, but whoso putteth his trust in the Lord shall be safe.

Proverbs 29:25

We in Phobics Victorious found fear to be our deadly enemy. Fear interfered with our ability to give and receive love. Fear kept us in bondage.

As we turn our focus to our Higher Power, Jesus, we are secure in His love for us. We are confident of who we are in Him. Fear of others leaves us. Pleasing God becomes more important than pleasing others. We learn to love man unconditionally and to walk in the freedom of God's love. We trust the Lord as our Divine Creator, who is faithful to do a good work in all who walk with Him.

Fear thou not, for I am with thee; be not dismayed; for I am Thy God; I will strengthen thee; yea, I will help thee.

Isaiah 41:10

Suffering phobics fear situations and people. They are locked into the physical realm. When we make contact with our Higher Power, we become aware of Spiritual reality.

Today, we will keep our focus on eternal realities. We will be aware of the presence of our Higher Power with us at all times. His Spirit will strengthen us in all our endeavors. We know His power exceeds all earthly powers.

January 5

Say to them that are of a fearful heart, Be strong, fear not; behold, your God will come with vengeance, even God with a recompense, He will come and save you.

Isaiah 35:4

I will practice faith instead of fear. When fearful thoughts enter my mind, I will resist them. I will divert my thinking to the ability of God to save me from destructive forces.

I will hold the higher vision, the broader view. There is a plan of good for my life. I will increase my faith and trust in God. I will let go and let God.

January 6

Thou wilt keep him in perfect peace, whose mind is stayed on thee; because he trusteth in thee.

Isaiah 26:3

We phobics can let outside influences destroy our peace of mind and serenity.

Today, I will trust in my Higher Power, in His wisdom and strength to bring peace into my fearful heart. I will be at peace, knowing His sovereignty over all and His love for all will prevail. I know we do not live in a haphazard universe and just as there is order in the universe, there is order in my life as long as I trust in Him.

Peace I leave with you, my peace I give unto you; not as the world giveth, give I unto you. Let not your heart be troubled, neither let it be afraid.

John 14:27

When we in Phobics Victorious take the third step and surrender our will and life to the care of our Higher Power, Jesus Christ, we are open and receptive to being filled with His peace.

Today, I will stop trying to compel things and people to go my way so I can feel in control of my life. My compulsion to control people, places and things, and my obstinate self-will, I release and let go. I am ready to be filled with peace, thus driving out fearful responses.

For God hath not given us the spirit of fear; but of power, and of love and of a sound mind.

II Timothy 1:7

We in Phobics Victorious had let fear be the ruling factor in our lives. This destructive emotion led to all kinds of problems, put us in bondage, and narrowed our perimeter.

Today, we refuse to let fear rule our lives. We turn to our Higher Power and surrender our lives to Him. We receive His power and His love which drives out fear. Through faith, belief and trust in our Higher Power, we are given a sound mind.

January 9

For ye have not received the spirit of bondage again to fear; but ye have received the Spirit of adoption.

Romans 8:15

Our Higher Power is our constant companion. When we turn to Him for help, He gives us His Spirit. The Spirit of the Twelve Step fellowship is not bound by time or space. It sets us free. It is powerful and loving.

Let us remember today that we are no longer in bondage to fear, but have accepted the free gift of our Higher Power's Spirit. We are part of a Spiritual family, a unity of love, beauty, peace, and freedom. We are healthy, whole, and free.

The Eternal God is your refuge, and underneath are the everlasting arms.

Deuteronomy 33:27

The devastating effects of acute panic attacks have left us terrified, unable to cope and function. We sought healing through physical, psychological, and spiritual means.

Let's never forget that our divine Creator, our Higher Power, is with us. He will not abandon us in this affliction. He gives us a safe refuge. He holds us in His arms. He is greater than illness and greater than death. Through our belief in and surrender to God, we receive that spiritual experience referred to in our twelfth step.

The Lord is my light and my salvation; whom shall I fear? The Lord is the strength of my life; of whom shall I be afraid?

Psalm 27:1

We in Phobics Victorious definitely know the word fear. We have found many things fearsome. We have found seemingly innocuous things fearsome.

Our acute panic attacks made us afraid of fear itself.

When we realize that faith is the opposite of fear and that fear is a bogey-man, a fake, we begin recovery. Today, I will have faith in my Higher Power. With the strength of my Higher Power filling me, I will be unafraid.

January 12

And deliver them who through fear of death were all their lifetime subject to bondage.

Hebrews 2:15

Today I will be fully aware that the Spirit of our Higher Power, that Spirit of our Twelve Step fellowship, transcends death. I will acknowledge that that Spirit is eternal, it is powerful and it is love.

Because we are also spiritual beings, we will become one with that Spirit when we surrender our will and our lives to our Higher Power. I will no longer fear death, for I know that in the power of the Spirit, I will overcome.

I will never leave thee nor forsake thee. The Lord is my helper, and I will not fear what man shall do unto me.

Hebrews 13:5-6

When I feel overwhelmed by my fears, by people and circumstances in my life, I will remember that my Higher Power has promised to never leave me. If I hold to faith in that promise and faith in His love for me and His ability to bring good out of disaster, strength out of weakness, then I will not be afraid what man can do to me. Through Him, I will have victory and freedom from fear. Thank You, Higher Power!

January 14

Casting all your care upon him; for He careth for you.

1 Peter 5:7

We in Twelve Step fellowships practice our program every day, one day at a time. We do not graduate, but continue our spiritual journey to serenity, light, peace and joy.

Today I will cast my cares upon my

Higher Power as I do each day. I will not carry a burden around on my shoulders when He says he will carry it. I will remember the great Burden Bearer and turn my fears over. I will also help to lighten the burden of my fellow Phobics Victorious members by sharing and caring.

January 15

There is no fear in love; but perfect love casteth out fear;

1 John 4:18

Fear is the deadly enemy of love. We phobics know that all too well. I will avoid fearful thoughts today and consciously replace them with thoughts of love.

Help me Higher Power to truly love others.

Help me to truly love You and to love myself. Show me Your love that I might love others without fear. Help me to not give place to fear, doubt, and confusion for these are false beliefs. Help me to replace my illusions with Truth.

0' that there were such an heart in them, that they would fear me, and keep all my commandments always, that it might be well with them, and with their children forever.

Deuteronomy 5:29

Today I will examine my moral self. I will take an honest inventory of my defects and assets. I will try to see where any defects of character may have increased my anxiety level. Where I see moral compromises, I will admit them, and be willing to do what is right. With the help of my Higher Power, I will become purer, holier, sanctified. I will not be afraid of man nor circumstances. I will have the peace that surpasseth human understanding.

Be strong and of a good courage, fear not, nor be afraid of them; for the Lord thy God, He it is that doth go with thee; He will not fail thee nor forsake thee.

Deuteronomy 31:6

In and of myself, I am powerless over

fear, but because my Higher Power is with me I will have strength. I believe that He will not fail me, nor forsake me. His power is greater than my fear and panic attacks and through my weaknesses He will make me strong. I have victory over my fear through my Higher Power, the Lord Jesus Christ. My victory is in Him, and He abides in me.

January 18

Yea, though I walk through the valley of the shadow of death, I will fear no evil, for thou art with me: thy rod and thy staff they comfort me.

Psalm 23:4

We in Phobics Victorious know all too well the debilitating, paralyzing effects of fear. We also know that we are faced with fear provoking situations — dangers, disease, death.

Yet today I will affirm the resurrection power of Christ, the good Shepherd. His power, the Higher Power in my life has already defeated fear, disease, and death. In His Spirit, we are free — free to live and free to love.

January 19

The angel of the Lord encampeth round about them that fear him, and delivereth them.

Psalm 34:7

Experiencing panic attacks has affected our whole outlook on life. We've viewed things through fear and depression.

Today, I will see that there is a power greater than this fear. This power is right near me and delivers me from the distorted view of the world that was precipitated by panic attacks. I will believe in and begin to see transformation in myself and my circumstances — a transformation from fear-filled to faith-filled, from negative to positive.

January 20

The Lord is on my side, I will not fear: What can man do unto me?

Psalm 118:6

Today I have faith in my Higher Power's love for me. I know I am created in His image and that His Spirit dwells in me. Because I yield my will to Him, He sanctifies me.

Nothing in my outside surroundings can harm me since the Spirit of the Lord dwells in me. Nothing that man can do overpowers the Higher Power within me. I will not be afraid.

January 21

Be not afraid of sudden fear, neither of the desolation of the wicked, when it cometh.

Proverbs 3:25

Today with our will surrendered to our Higher Power's will, we will not be afraid. Our Higher Power is in charge of the outcome. Because His Spirit abides in us and because we choose to abide in Him, we can go through any negative circumstances victoriously.

We know that we are not alone because we are surrendered to Him. When all around us, there is wickedness and desolation, we will remain unafraid and will overcome.

Let us hear the conclusion of the whole matter: Fear God, and keep his commandments; for this is the whole duty of man.

Ecclesiastes 12:13

We found in Phobics Victorious that all our own efforts at controlling our panic attacks were futile, or at best, half-way measures. We could dull the anxiety with medication or alcohol, or we could hide and avoid people and things, but this wasn't freedom.

Today, we practice righteous fear of the Lord or respect for His guidelines to life. As we strive to keep His commandments, we find we are less and less afraid. We know we are right with God.

In righteousness shalt thou be established; thou shalt be far from oppression; for thou shalt not fear; and from terror; for it shall not come near thee.

Isaiah 54:14

We Phobics have lived a life, governed by fear. We saw no way out. Today I will keep my focus on God. I will ask myself "Am I right with God?" I know that if I am righteous or am willing to be righteous, then He will stabilize me. I will not be a victim of the oppression of panic attacks and phobias. In my safe place of rightness with my Higher Power, terror will not come near me.

January 24

But when Jesus heard, He answered him, saying, Fear not; believe only, and she shall be made whole.

Luke 8:50

Today I take the second step and come to believe that my Higher Power will restore me to wholeness. I know that wholeness means freedom from debilitating fears and anxieties.

Higher Power, please show me how to believe. Help me when doubts and confusion enter into my thoughts. Lord, just as I believe in Your power over disease, nature, and death, I believe in Your power to heal me and make me whole. Thank You, Higher Power!

But even the very hairs of your head are all numbered. Fear not therefore; ye are of more value than many sparrows.

Luke 12:7

Today I will remember that I am a child of God created in His image. His knowledge of me is so detailed that he even knows how many hairs I have on my head. I need not fear that my condition is unknown to Him. Just as the creatures of Nature, the birds, the flowers, the animals all are in sync with the outworkings of life in the universe, I can be assured that if I accept His love and His will for me and if I follow Him, my life will reflect harmony and peace.

January 26

Fear not, little flock; for it is your Father's good pleasure to give you the kingdom.

Luke 12:32

I will realize today that if I go it alone and try to figure out my phobias myself, that I will only fail. I will be conscious of the life that my Higher Power is offering me, for it is a gift. All I have to do is accept it.

I will cease to struggle today to solve my problems, phobias, panic attacks. I will stop doing. I will quiet my mind and be still. I will receive this gift of life. Today I will just be.

January 27

Fear not; for thou shalt not be ashamed; neither be thou confounded; for thou shalt not be put to shame; for thou shalt forget the shame of thy youth.

Isaiah 54:4

Many of us in Phobics Victorious, experienced our first phobias and panic attacks in youth. We felt inadequate, embarrassed, and ashamed. We tried to cover-up our feelings of insecurity and outright terror.

Our Higher Power has promised us that not only will we be free of shame, but we will even forget the shame of our youth. I will reflect on the magnitude of His promise. This means total freedom from the past.

*And it shall come to pass in the day,
that, the Lord shall give thee rest from
thy sorrow, and from thy fear, and from
the hard bondage wherein thou wast
made to serve.*

Isaiah 14:3

What a promise! My Higher Power has
said that He will give me rest from this
fear and sorrow, from this bondage. I no
longer need to be a prisoner in my own
house — I am free from racing heartbeat,
paralysis, and cold, numbing fear.

Today, I will live by faith in this
promise. My hope is in the Lord and
in the faithfulness of His word. I will
not buy into fear nor give place to its
debilitating effects. I will see it for what
it is — a hoax, a lie.

January 29

Come unto me, all ye that labour and are heavy laden and I will give you rest. Take my yoke upon you, and learn of me; for I am meek and lowly in heart; and ye shall find rest unto your souls. For my yoke is easy, and my burden is light.

Matthew 11:28-30

Having fought the affliction of fear, phobias and panic attacks, in exhaustion, I bring myself to my Higher Power. Today, I will rest at His feet. I will shift my focus from myself to Him. My soul needs a vacation from stress. He has promised rest. I will learn about Him, so I can have His peace and serenity. I will stop rushing to find this or that cure, but will reflect upon Him.

January 30

Let your light so shine before man, that they may see your good works, and glorify your Father which is in Heaven.

Matthew 5:16

In the past I have allowed fear to block the light I can shine before men. Today, I will replace that fear with faith in my

Higher Power and in myself. I will let my light shine, for I know my Higher Power fills me with His spirit. His spirit dispels the fear in me and overcomes the handicaps I have suffered, allowing me to begin to help others. I will trust in Him today.

January 31

But I say unto you, Love your enemies, bless them that curse you, do good to them that hate you, and pray for them which despitefully use you and persecute you.
Matthew 5:44

Today, I will be at peace with all men. I will let go of any past hurts and resentments. I will forgive those who have harmed me, and I will forgive myself for past mistakes.

When I truly love everyone, I know I will be without fear. I will have compassion on other imperfect human beings, for we are all imperfect, striving to grow.

February 1

Take therefore no thought for the morrow; for the morrow shall take thought for the things of itself. Sufficient unto the day is the evil thereof.

Matthew 6:34

Today is a gift to live the best I can. By living fully today, I lose my fear of past poor mistakes or of future calamities.

There are no guarantees regarding tomorrow, so I will choose to live abundantly today. Worry and fear over yesterday or tomorrow only burden me today. So I let these go, and I let God direct my life.

February 2

Ask, and it shall be given you; seek, and ye shall find; knock, and it shall be opened unto you.

Matthew 7:7

Today, I will believe these promises: that if I ask, I will receive and if I seek, I will find. As a recovering phobic, I ask for freedom from fear and from the often accompanying depression. I ask for freedom from the negative habit patterns and addictions that arose out of my fear and panic attacks. I give thanks for my new life of faith and trust. I praise and glorify my Higher Power through this personal transformation in my life.

February 3

They that be whole need not a physician, but they that are sick.

Matthew 9:12

Jesus is the Great Physician, powerful enough to heal us from disease and to deliver us from bondage. We with phobias, panic attacks and subsequent depression have indeed been sick. Often our behavior at camouflaging our fears and avoiding life made us even sicker. How thankful we are today that our Higher Power, Jesus, has come to make us whole. We know His Spirit is more powerful than fear, and we welcome His Spirit, and ask Him to abide with us.

February 4

Why are ye fearful, 0 ye of little faith?
Matthew 8:26

Today, I will ask God to change me from — little to big faith — I will walk by faith; faith that God is good, that He is just, that I am His child and that He loves me. I will not be afraid of calamity of any kind. I will not give in to doubt.

Today, I choose to follow my Higher Power, Jesus Christ. He will set me free from the bondage of fear and its repercussions. Thank You, Jesus, for the calm this brings to me and to those I love.

February 5

The harvest truly is plentious, but the labourers are few; Pray ye therefore the Lord of the harvest, that he will send forth labourers into his harvest.

Matthew 9:37-38

Today we will carry the message of the Twelve Steps of Phobics Victorious to other suffering phobics. We will share our experience, strength and hope. We will show how our lives have been transformed by our surrender to our Higher Power. We will be lights shining in the darkness of fear, disease and death. We will live today as overcomers, by practicing the principles of Phobics Victorious in all our affairs.

Heal the sick, cleanse the lepers, raise the dead, cast out devils; freely ye have received, freely give.

Matthew 10:8

Little do we know the power of living faith. Our lives have been so consumed by fear that we could not see beyond it. But today, again, our Higher Power, Jesus Christ, empowers us through the authority and power of His Holy Spirit. Our Higher Power freely gives us this gift of His life and Spirit, if we but surrender to Him. Today I surrender again to Him. I turn my will and life over to His care. I will follow Jesus. I will freely give this hope to other phobics.

And there arose a great storm of wind, and the waves beat into the ship, so that it was now full and he was in the hinder part of the ship, asleep on a pillow, and they awake him and say unto him, Master, carest thou not that we perish? And he arose, and rebuked the wind, and said unto the sea, "Peace, be still," and the wind ceased and there was a great calm. And he said unto them, "Why are ye so fearful? How is it that ye have no faith?"

Mark 4:37-40

Today I have faith in the power of God as revealed through Jesus Christ. I know that with His Spirit dwelling in me that I, too, have power. I will increase my faith and not give place to fear. Through the authority and power of Jesus Christ in me, I am delivered from fear.

February 8

And fear not them which kill the body, but are not able to kill the soul; but rather fear him which is able to destroy both soul and body in hell.

Matthew 10:28

It is my vertical relationship with my Higher Power that directly influences the horizontal relationships in my life. Today, I will seek to get right with God. I will examine my behavior honestly. I will be willing to let go of all defects of character that keep me from experiencing the fullness of God, of life and love. I will grow more Christlike.

Are not two sparrows sold for a farthing? And one of them shall not fall on the ground without your Father. But the very hairs of your head are all numbered. Fear ye not therefore, ye are of more value than many sparrows.

Matthew 10:29

I will remember that I am a child of God. He created me and is concerned about me. He draws me to Himself with loving kindness and patience. He forgives my errors. He promises to never leave me nor forsake me. He will complete the transforming work in me so that I will reflect His beauty, truth and love. I am valuable to Him.

February 10

The Son of man came eating and drinking, and they say, Behold a man gluttonous and a winebibber, a friend of publicans and sinners.

Matthew 11:19

I am confident of my Higher Power's love for me and for all men, no matter what our mistakes and errors. He understands our weaknesses, that we are flesh. He knows we need His Spirit for guidance and strength. He knows how we are held captive by fear. He gives liberty to those who trust Him.

My Higher Power knows my feelings of fear and has compassion for me. Through faith in Christ, I am set free.

February 11

And when the disciples saw him walking on the sea, they were troubled, saying, it is a spirit; and they cried out for fear. But straightway Jesus spoke unto them, saying, Be of good cheer; it is I; be not afraid.
Matthew 14:26

Today, I reflect on the mighty power of God. I need not be afraid. With my Higher Power with me, I am able to overcome obstacles. I remember that in my own strength alone, I can do nothing. But with God all things are possible.

I invite my Higher Power again today to empower me. I receive His power.

And he said, Come, and when Peter was come down out of the ship, he walked on the water, to go to Jesus. But when he saw the wind boisterous, he was afraid; and beginning to sink, he cried, saying, Lord, save me. And immediately Jesus stretched forth his hand and caught him, and said unto him, O thou of little faith, wherefore didst thou doubt.

Matthew 14:29-31

I will not give place to doubt and confusion. My mind is strictly focused on my Higher Power, Jesus. It is my faith in Him that allows me to rise above all seeming disturbances. When I fear and doubt, I flounder and become immobile. With faith, I can do all things.

Not that which goeth into the mouth defileth a man, but that which cometh out of the mouth, this defileth a man.

Matthew 15:11

Today I will not judge men by what they wear, or what they eat or drink, nor by where they live nor by their role, religion, occupation. These are all externals. I will know and believe that what is important is what comes from the heart and mind.

I will keep my thoughts clean and positive. I will keep my heart loving and soft and compassionate. If the inside of me is holy, then light will be reflected out of me in spite of external conditions. I will be true and honest today.

February 14

For what is a man profited if he shall gain the whole world, and lose his own soul?
Matthew 16:26

Because we have been so dominated by our fears and insecurities, we in Phobics Victorious have found a myriad of ways to manipulate people and things in order to gain security.

But today I will acknowledge that the negative ways I've handled my fears — perhaps through addictions to money, drugs and alcohol, sex, dependent relationships, or acquiring material possessions are all unhealthy for me. They only keep me in a form of bondage. I will concentrate on recovering from the soul-sickness of fear and depression through my Higher Power and the Twelve Step program.

February 15

If ye have faith as a grain of mustard seed, ye shall say unto this mountain, Remove hence to yonder place; and it shall remove; and nothing shall be impossible unto you.

Matthew 17:20

I replace all fearful thoughts with faith thoughts. I have faith and trust in my Higher Power's will for my life. I know He loves me and that He is faithful to keep His promises. I know that I am a child of God, that He is my Heavenly Father. He sees the end from the beginning, and His divine plan for me will bring goodness, and beauty and love. With faith in Him, I will overcome fear. As I give Him my weaknesses, I will become strong.

February 16

For the Son of Man is come to save that which was lost.

Matthew 18:11

Because fear has been such a destructively powerful emotion in our lives, we became alienated from life. We were in despair and sometimes in death's grip. We became lost. But when we turned to our Higher Power, we found that He is here to save us.

Today, again, as I do each day, I turn to Jesus, my Higher Power, to save me. I have been lost, outside the safety of His fold. He, the Shepherd, brings me into His fold, and I am safe and free from fear.

February 17

For where two or three are gathered together in my name, there am I in the midst of them.

Matthew 18:20

We in Phobics Victorious know that in the midst of our meetings is Jesus, our Higher Power. His spirit is strong to heal us and make us whole.

I will fellowship with other believers and will help the newcomer in our group meetings. In Your name, I can help others find freedom from fear. Thank You, Jesus, for your healing presence among us. Thank You for setting me free from fear. I can always count on You!

February 18

Verily I say unto you, If ye have faith, and doubt not, ye shall not only do this which is done to the fig tree, but also if ye shall say unto this mountain, Be thou removed, and be thou cast into the sea, it shall be done.

Matthew 21:21

Fear causes doubt, and doubt paralyzes us. I will not give place to fear and doubt today. I choose to live confidently, courageously, and positively. I know I can do all things through Jesus Christ who strengthens me. Without Him, I can do nothing. So I walk in the power of His Spirit, and I live lovingly, abundantly, and freely.

February 19

And all things, whatsoever ye shall ask in prayer, believing, ye shall receive.

Matthew 21:22

Today, Higher Power, I believe that You love me. I believe that I am a Child of God, created in His image. I believe that

You want me to have Your joy and love and holiness. I ask, Higher Power, that You deliver me from fear and depression. I ask for Your power in me and for Your will to be done in my life. I ask for freedom to love. I ask for reconciliation in all relationships where fear has caused broken fellowship. Thank You!

February 20

Watch and pray, that ye enter not into temptation; the spirit indeed is willing, but the flesh is weak.

Matthew 26:41

We know that we have compromised our standards many times by fulfilling our needs for love and security with unwholesome behavior. Today we replace our fear of unmet needs with faith and trust in our Higher Power's will for our lives.

I will try to make healthy choices. I will remember love is better than hate, good better than evil. I will resist temptations that ultimately destroy me. I pray, Higher Power, that You will help me.

Then, said Jesus unto them, Be not afraid; go tell my brethren that they go into Galilee, and there shall they see me.

Matthew 28:10

We know that through our Higher Power, Jesus Christ, we can be overcomers. Through His resurrection, Jesus overcame death. Today, we will remember that Jesus told us we would have tribulations in this world, but for us to be of good cheer for He has overcome the world. He knows that we can be very afraid. By reflecting on His overcoming miracles of healing diseases, casting out demons, subduing nature and rising from the grave, we will have faith in our ability, through Christ in us, to also overcome.

All power is given unto me in heaven and in earth.

Matthew 28:18

Just imagine, all power in heaven and earth given to Jesus, our Higher Power. And just think, He offers us that power as a free gift. Today, we will accept and receive the gift of Jesus Christ. He says He will give us living water, that we will never thirst. He tells us that He and His Father will dwell in us through the Holy Spirit. If we but believe in Him and His power to restore us to sanity, we will be healthy, whole and free.

February 23

And lo, I am with you always, even unto the end of the world.

Matthew 28:20

We do not have a Higher Power who only stays for awhile or who will leave us in the middle of our recovery from fear. We have a Higher Power who has promised to be with us always.

When we start to doubt, lose faith, or give in to fear and despair, we will quickly think of our Higher Power's promise. He is faithful and true; He loves us. We will not let our fear and mistakes separate us from Him. We turn to Him again today, as we do each day.

Daughter, thy faith hath made thee whole; go in peace, and be whole of thy plague.

Mark 5:34

When we are so consumed by fear, panic attacks, and phobias, we lose sight of any faith in ourselves and in God. Many of us don't hold a loving picture of God because of past abuse by others. We view Him as punishing and severe. But faith is the opposite of fear. Because faith is a godly emotion, it can defeat fear.

Today, I will increase my faith in my Higher Power's ability to heal me of my affliction. I will also pray that my Higher Power will help me increase my faith.

As soon as Jesus heard the word that was spoken, he saith unto the ruler of the synagogue, Be not afraid, only believe.

Mark 5:36

We need to note that it is immediately after admitting our powerlessness over fear that we are led in Step Two to believe in a Higher Power. For our healing and recovery to be completed, we need to believe. It sounds so simple, yet it can be hard.

Today I will keep it simple by affirming, "I believe in You, Higher Power, that You can restore me to wholeness. I believe that I will be free of fear and panic attacks so that I can enjoy the joyful, carefree, spontaneity of youth."

February 26

Jesus said unto him, If thou canst believe, all things are possible to them that believeth.

Mark 9:23

Many of us have believed that we ourselves could find the cure and freedom from fear and panic attacks. We believed that psychiatrists could cure us. We did find some symptom relieving help through medications and psychotherapy techniques. But through the spiritual approach of our twelve steps, we find freedom from fear.

I choose to believe that I am being set free from fear. I believe I can do all things through Jesus Christ who strengthens me.

Have faith in God, For verily I say unto you, that whosoever shall say unto this mountain, Be thou removed and be thou cast into the sea; and shall not doubt in his heart, but shall believe that those things which he saith shall come to pass; he shall have whatsoever he saith.

Mark 11:22,23

God is not the author of confusion and doubt, nor did He give us a spirit of fear. Therefore, I will not let doubt exist in my mind. I believe that I can replace doubting thoughts immediately with believing and faith-filled thoughts. When I find myself dwelling on doubtful ideas, I will stop. I will shift my attention to my Higher Power.

February 28

The Spirit of the Lord is upon me, because he hath anointed me to preach the gospel to the poor; he hath sent me to heal the brokenhearted, to preach deliverance to the captives, and recovering of sight to the blind, to set at liberty them that are bruised.

Luke 4:18

Many of us have felt that fear, phobias, and panic attacks kept us prisoners. Some of us were literally bound to our own homes, afraid to go out. We did not have liberty to fully experience life.

Today, I will rest assured that my Higher Power, Jesus, will liberate me from the captivity I have been in. I thank You, Jesus, for delivering me from fear.

February 29

And the Lord God called unto Adam, and said unto him, Where art thou? And he said, I heard thy voice in the garden, and I was afraid, because I was naked, and I hid myself.
Genesis 3:9-10

Through disobedience to the divine will of God, man becomes aware of sin and evil and becomes afraid.

In my recovery from fear, I will take an honest inventory of my past and present behaviors.

I will admit where I did wrong. I will try to clean up my life and to get rid of past garbage. I find that the less I have to feel guilty about or be ashamed of, the greater confidence I have to meet life's situations. I can freely look others in the eye.

March 1

In God I will praise his word, in God I have put my trust; I will not fear what flesh can do unto me.

Psalm 56:4

Many of us feared other people — what they thought of us, if we measured up, or if we would be rejected or abandoned. We feared being left alone. We feared being hurt. When we put our trust in others we were often disappointed, and afraid.

My trust is in God alone, because He loves me. He is always with me; He will never leave me nor forsake me. He has the power to work in me to help me overcome all fleshly afflictions. I am a Child of God, created in His image, wholly and dearly loved.

March 2

No man, having put his hand to the plough, and looking back, is fit for the kingdom of God.

Luke 9:62

The journey of the Twelve Steps is a spiritual journey where we choose, one day at a time, to keep going on. Sometimes we get bogged down by looking back at the past or relapsing into past behaviors. But we start again, realizing we are only human, and that it takes time to change.

Once I begin this spiritual journey, I will not turn back. I will follow my Higher Power, Jesus.

March 3

And he said unto them, I beheld Satan as lightning falls from heaven. Behold, I give unto you power to tread on serpents and scorpions, and over all the power of the enemy; and nothing shall by any means hurt you.

Luke 10:18-19

Not only does our Higher Power have all power in heaven and earth, but also He gives us power. We must believe that He exists and have faith and trust in Him.

Fear, a deadly power of the enemy, is overcome through the power given me by my Higher Power. Today, I will reaffirm that this power is greater in me than the enemy, fear. The victory is won.

From whence cometh my help? My help cometh from the Lord, who made heaven and earth.

Psalm 121:1,2

We are God's creatures. He made us and understands our frailties. He desires us to grow into His likeness as children grow to emulate their parents. Therefore, He will help us mature and grow each day.

Today, I come again to my Higher Power for help in my affliction. I give Him my problems. I rest in Him and receive His peace.

And lead us not into temptation, but deliver us from evil.

Luke 11:4

Evil is such a strong force that we need deliverance from it. Fear has been an evil in our lives, leading us into all kinds of self-destructive thoughts and behaviors. We've been tempted to deal with fear through a variety of manipulations, even when it means compromising our standards.

My prayer today, Higher Power, is for deliverance from the evil of fear. Fill me with Your Holy Spirit to guide and direct my path. Teach me how to walk with Thee.

March 6

If you continue in my word, you are truly my disciples, and you will know the truth, and the truth will make you free.
John 8:31,32

Our Higher Power, Jesus, says He will meet us in His word and lead us to truly be his followers. His word will set us free to walk through life, fearless and rejoicing.

Today I meditate upon thy Word in the Holy Scriptures. I will practice Step Eleven to improve my conscious contact with God. It is my desire to know the truth and to be free.

March 7

I am the light of the world; Whoever follows me will never walk in darkness, but will have the light of life.
John 8:12

We in Phobics Victorious follow Jesus.

As we follow Him we journey from darkness into light Our worlds were dark through the intense fear we experienced. Now we see a way. There is light at the end of the tunnel.

Today, I choose to walk toward the light ever increasing glory. I will avoid the darkness of fear and depression.

March 8

With God all things are possible.
Matthew 19:26

Fears, phobias, panic attacks have seemed overwhelmingly impossible to deal with. They've often led to despair and depression. But we know there is recovery in the Twelve Step program.

Today, I acknowledge that nothing is too difficult nor impossible for my Higher Power to fix. I will give my "impossibles" to Him. I will trust Him, for He is faithful.

And without faith, it is impossible to please God, because anyone who comes to Him must believe that He exists and that He rewards those who earnestly seek Him.

Hebrews 11:6

Our lives have been devastated by fears and phobias. We lived by fear, not faith; we lost sight of hope. But today we come to our Higher Power in faith.

I know and affirm that my Higher Power exists! I know He cares for me more than I care about myself. He holds me close and heals my fears. I will seek Him earnestly today.

March 10

I am the vine; you are the branches. If a man remains in me and I in him, he will bear much fruit; apart from me you can do nothing.

John 15:5

We have discovered that we are powerless by ourselves to control our fear and panic. We've been able to mask the symptoms, but unable to break free of the affliction.

Today, I will believe that my Higher Power is with me and in me. I am healed. I will remember that on my own, I can do nothing. Where the Spirit is, there is freedom. I pray, today, to be filled with the Spirit. Thank You, Lord.

March 11

For the Lord is good; his steadfast love endures forever, and his faithfulness to all generations.

Psalm 100:5

God gives us patterns of His faithfulness throughout His creation — the cycles of the seasons; the ocean's waves; the sun, moon and stars — that same faithfulness is mine. Today, I receive You, Higher Power. I receive Your love. I surrender my life to You.

Even when there are setbacks or when appearances seem difficult, I will contemplate that You God are good, that You love me, and that You are faithful to me and those who will follow you.

I tell you the truth, unless a man is born again, he cannot see the kingdom of God.

                                            John 3:3

We know how much trouble our flesh gives us. Panic attacks have racked our bodies with all sorts of horrible symptoms. Many of us would have preferred death than to endure the bodily symptoms of panic attacks.

But just as we were physically born in the flesh and the body, we can be spiritually born. In this new birth, our spiritual bodies can not fail. Today, I choose to concentrate on my spiritual birth and growth.

For God so loved the world that he gave his one and only Son, that whoever believes in him shall not perish but have everlasting life.

                                           John 3:16

Many of us in Phobics Victorious have felt close to perishing. Our symptoms and discomfort made death appear imminent. Today, I know that God loved me so deeply, that He provided a way out of my suffering. He gave Jesus, my Higher Power, to restore me to wholeness and sanity — I will get well. My Higher Power gives me life and freedom. Everywhere I look, I see people working the spiritual program of the Twelve Steps and recovering.

March 14

Fear not, little flock; for it is your Father's good pleasure to give you the kingdom.
Luke 12:32

Sometimes we've been so beaten down by our fears and panic attacks that we lost sight of our Higher Power's love for us. God does not want us to suffer. We are His children, and He wants to give us all that is good.

Let me examine my life today to see when and how I have separated myself from the love of God. Perhaps willful sin, disobedience, lack of belief, and doubt have contributed to my condition. Higher Power, sanctify me that I may dwell in Your presence.

*Verily I say unto you, Whosoever shall
not receive the kingdom of God as a little
child shall in no wise enter therein.*

Luke 18:17

Fear is the opposite of faith. Our panic
attacks left us so stricken that we were
immobilized by fear.

Today, I replace fear with the simple
faith of a child, faith in my Higher
Power. As a child implicitly trusts those
who love him, I will trust in God. He will
not fail me. He cares about me. He has
promised to always be with me. Lord,
gently lead me, as a father guides a child.

*And take heed to yourselves, lest at any
time your heart be overcharged with surfeit-
ing and drunkenness, and cares of this life,
and so that day come upon you unawares.*

Luke 21:34

Many of us have sought to camouflage
our fears through alcohol. Some of us
became unhealthily dependent on mood
altering drugs.

I will observe myself carefully today to

see if I am using alcohol or drugs, rather than changing my life with Christ's help. I will depend on God to deliver me from my fears.

March 17

But whosoever drinketh of the water that I shall give him shall never thirst; but the water that I shall give him shall be in him a well of water springing up into everlasting life.

John 4:14

We in Phobics Victorious must come to our Higher Power, Jesus Christ, and receive His gift of living water. Only then will our needs be met.

I will not thirst today over worldly concerns; I will receive the water of life from Jesus. In Him, I have life abundant. I live fully and joyfully with power and strength.

March 18

Ye worship ye know not what; we know what we worship for salvation is of the Jews.
John 4:22

Our fears and our sins, our guilt and our remorse are tied closely together.

Before we met Jesus, our Higher Power, our lives were filled with confusion and fear. We felt alone, unloved and afraid. It is through Jesus Christ, our Higher Power, that we are saved.

Thank You, Jesus, for being a Saviour whom we can know and worship. You set us free from panic attacks and paralysis. Your Spirit helps us overcome.

March 19

I am the bread of life; he that cometh to me shall never hunger; and he that believeth in me shall never thirst.

John 6:35

Jesus, I once hungered for inner peace and a feeling of safety. My panic attacks created a terrifying emptiness inside. You filled my starving spirit and brought health and joy to my heart.

Today I will feed on You and trust You to give me the confidence I crave.

March 20

If any man thirst, let him come unto me, and drink.

John 7:37

I come to You, Jesus, the water of life. I bring to You all my imperfections and errors. I place them at the cross. I bury with Christ all my old fearful ways. I rise with Christ in victory. With His Spirit in me, I am unafraid. I will never thirst again. Thank You for Your promise, Jesus!

March 21

I am the light of the world; he that followeth me shall not walk in darkness, but shall have the light of life.

John 8:12

With fear in control, many of us isolated ourselves. We were afraid to go out, afraid to participate in life.

Our Higher Power, Jesus, has brought us into the light. My vision is no longer darkened by fear. I desire the brilliant sunshine to light every corner of my heart. I accept Your power today!

March 22

If ye continue in my word, then ye are my disciples indeed; And ye shall know the truth, and the truth shall make you free.

John 8:31

Freedom from fear is our desire. Today, I will reflect on this promise from our Higher Power, Jesus Christ. He tells us that we will be set free if we continue in His word.

I will be His disciple today. I will read God's word and meditate on its truths. I know that He is faithful to fulfill His promises.

March 23

If the Son therefore shall make you free, ye shall be free indeed.
John 8:36

We have learned many ways to deal with our phobias and panic attacks, some constructive ways, some destructive ways.

Today, I will receive the promise of complete freedom. I receive it, because it is a gift from my Higher Power, Jesus Christ. Thank You, Jesus, for setting me free. As I have freely received, I will freely give through the Twelve Step fellowship of Phobics Victorious.

Verily, verily, I say unto you, Before Abraham was, I Am.

John 8:58

When we in Phobics Victorious proclaim Jesus Christ as our Higher Power, we are not referring only to the man, Jesus who lived on earth, we are referring to the Son of God who transcends time and space.

Let us be conscious of the miraculous power of Christ, a power far stronger than fear and panic attacks. He formed the world, He hung the stars in space. His power is ours for the asking if we will believe.

I am the door; by me if any man enter in, he shall be saved, and shall go in and out, and find pasture.

John 10:9

Many of us have cried out to be saved from our fears. We are like sheep who cannot find our way home. We need to be saved from our loneliness and gloom.

I look to my Higher Power, Jesus, who

was and is victorious over all this. He gives me His Spirit so I too can go in and out of my home safely. Today, I remember that I am not alone in my quest to overcome. He is with me always.

March 26

I am come that they might have life, and that they might have it more abundantly.
John 10:10

Our lives became narrow and confined. We were prisoners of fear, too afraid to enjoy life.

My Higher Power came to earth to give me life abundant. With my eyes on Jesus, and His Spirit dwelling in me, I rise above earthly, fleshly confinements. I see the bigger picture. I feel the love of God in the fellowship of Phobics Victorious.

March 27

This sickness is not unto death, but for the glory of God that the Son of God might be glorified thereby.

John 11:4

We know that there is victory over illness and disease through Jesus our

Higher Power As we continue our spiritual walk today, let us remember that it is in our recovery that our Higher Power is glorified.

Today, I receive Your healing power, Your life, Your light and Your spirit. Work through me and allow Your glory to shine through me. Dispel the cloud of fear. Thank you!

March 28

I am the resurrection, and the life: he that believeth in me, though dead, yet shall he live. And whosoever liveth and believeth in me shall never die. Believest thou this?

John 11:25,26

We Phobics are often so paralyzed by fear, that we feel like living corpses. Jesus, our Higher Power, can revive us, calling us to resurrection power.

Help me today to give any fear or phobia to You, Jesus, that I may walk and leap for joy in Your name.

I am come a light into the world, that whosoever believeth on me should not abide in darkness.

John 12:46

Many phobics stay isolated in dark enclosed places, afraid to venture out into the light. In sheer desperation, some sought out counselors. Some became suicidal. Some have even taken their lives. We deal with a life and death situation.

Today I turn to the great Counselor, our Higher Power, the Lord Jesus Christ. I invite Him into my heart. His light will dispel my fears, so that I will no longer stay hidden in darkness. He will flood my life with light.

A new commandment I give unto you, That ye love one another; as I have loved you, that ye also love one another.

John 13:34

Fear is a great enemy of love. It paralyzes us, leaving us too immobilized to reach out to others in love.

Today, I will practice this new commandment. I will take the risk to love. It is my choice. I will not only love those who love me, but I will also love those who have hurt me. Give me courage, Higher Power, to love as you love.

March 31

Jesus saith unto him, I am the way, the truth and the life; no man cometh unto the Father but by me.

John 14:6

We in Phobics Victorious come to the cross. We have tried many other ways to overcome our phobias. Jesus, our Burden Bearer, is the way to peace, joy and freedom. He is the truth we long for. Through Him, we have access to life. I am free from sin, disease, and death through the resurrection power of the Lord Jesus Christ. I walk in newness of life — healthy, whole, and free.

April 1

Let not your heart be troubled: ye believe in God, believe also in me.

John 14:1

Jesus, our Higher Power, knows we often worry and fret that the worst possible thing may happen. He says not to let our heart be troubled.

Today, I believe in God and His Son Jesus Christ I believe Jesus came into this world to save us. I believe that He is restoring me to sanity, to wholeness. Thank You, Higher Power.

April 2

And whatsoever ye shall ask in my name, that will I do, that the Father may be glorified in the Son.

John 14:13

Dear Heavenly Father, in the name of Thy Son Jesus Christ, I ask that You deliver me from fear, phobia and panic attacks. I believe that if I ask in Your name, You will heal me.

Today, I receive the gift of life. I receive God's love and His healing power. I claim the courage to conduct my life free of fear. I will glorify God through my new behavior. I am filled with thy Holy Spirit.

April 3

But the Comforter, which is the Holy Ghost, whom the Father will send in my name, he shall teach you all things.

John 14:26

We in Phobics Victorious, need to remember that the Holy Spirit will guide us and teach us.

Help me be less demanding on myself, and others, for getting what I want right now. Teach me to trust in my Higher Power and rest in the guidance of His Spirit. Remind me, when I impulsively fight to control things my way, to let go of my desires. I surrender my will to Him.

April 4

Seek the Lord, and His strength; Seek His face evermore.

Psalm 105:4

In Phobics Victorious, we are on a spiritual journey. Each day, one day at a time, we choose to follow Jesus. Each morning, we take our third step, surrendering our wills and lives over to the care of our Higher Power. We do not work the Twelve Steps only when we feel like it, but rather, every single day, we continue to grow and develop spiritually.

This day, I look to Jesus. I desire to do His will for me. In all that surrounds me, in all I do, I pray to see the Lord.

April 5

Abide in me and I in you.

John 15:4

When we abide in our Higher Power, Jesus, and He abides in us, we are not alone. We do not have to fear. His power is sufficient for us.

Abiding in Him, He can turn my weaknesses to strengths. I can then reach out to others, to help them be healed as He healed me. I accept him today, and let His light shine through me.

April 6

If ye abide in me, and my words abide in you, ye shall ask what ye will, and it shall be done unto you.

John 15:7

Being so fearful, we in Phobics Victorious acquired faulty belief systems. Our acute fear symptoms blocked out our ability to have faith and trust.

Today I will abide in Jesus, knowing His truth makes me free. Fear is not of God. It is a lie, a deception. I will ask Jesus, my Higher Power, to heal me and set me free.

April 7

In the world ye shall have tribulation: but be of good cheer; I have overcome the world.
John 16:33

Tribulation enters the world of we phobics at every turn. We fear people and places and even fear itself. We will cheerfully trust in our Higher Power, Jesus Christ. He overcame disease and death. He won the victory over fear, temptation and evil.

I will look to Jesus when I get fearful or discouraged. He will help me overcome my fears.

April 8

Take every thought captive to obey Christ.
II Corinthians 10:5

Our thoughts have been so adversely

affected by fear. Fear is a false belief, a delusion. Fear immobilized and paralyzed us.

Today, I will guard my thoughts. I will stop the fear thoughts. I will stop the thoughts that are destructive and wrong. I will reflect on the word of God in the Holy Scriptures. In my thoughts and actions, I will obey.

April 9

Behold, God is my helper, the Lord is the upholder of my life.

Psalm 54:4

We have sought so many ways to deal with our fears: denying them, masking them, medicating them through addictions and compulsions.

Today, I face my fears. I give them to God. He is my helper. He will deliver me and keep me safe. In Him is life everlasting. He promises to be with me always.

April 10

He spoke to them of the kingdom of God, and cured those who had need of healing.

Luke 9:11

We need to be healed of our inaccurate

perceptions of life, of our phobias and acute panic attacks. They have given us a deep sense of loss and alienation.

In the kingdom of God, we are forever united in the love of the Spirit. Our Higher Power heals us of all fear. Today, I accept that love. I am filled with the love of God.

April 11

Be strong and of good courage; be not frightened, neither be dismayed; for the Lord your God is with you wherever you go.
Joshua 1:9

Often, because of fear, we have allowed ourselves to live life passively — a life of avoidance and isolation. Too afraid to speak up for ourselves, too afraid of abandonment, we allowed others to victimize or exploit us.

Today, I will be fully conscious of who I am — a Child of God. I will boldly confront where needed. I will use discernment and wisdom with people who take advantage of my fear.

And I shall walk at liberty, for I have sought thy precepts.

Psalm 119:45

After we have made our searching and fearless moral inventory in Step Four, we are more aware of our defects of character. We become willing to let God remove our shortcomings. Along with that, we are joyfully surprised to feel so free.

I am liberated from fear as I seek to follow God's precepts. If I fall back into fearful thinking, I will examine my thoughts and actions to be sure they are right, true, and honest.

April 13

In God, whose word I praise, in God I trust without a fear.

Psalm 56:4

Our Higher Power, Jesus Christ, has promised to never leave us nor forsake us. He can do in us what we cannot do ourselves.

Today, His word I praise. In His written word we read that He heals our diseases. He casts out demons. He raises the dead. He is risen. He is alive, and His spirit dwells in me.

April 14

Fear not, stand firm, and see the salvation of the Lord.

Exodus 14:13

Fear has kept us far away from many things: other people, places, experiences and even from knowing our Higher Power — from feeling His love. Fear has alienated us from our true selves, but God can cast out fear.

As we accept Jesus Christ as our Higher Power, as our personal Savior, we are brought right in to the throne of God. He can cast out fear. He can make us stand firm. We can conquer our phobias through the salvation of the Lord.

April 15

Have faith in God.

Mark 11:22

Today I will exercise greater faith in my Higher Power, Jesus Christ. I bring my fears, doubts, despairs to the foot of the cross. I leave them there.

He is my burden bearer. He delivers me

from fear. He reconciles me to God, myself, and others. He promises that my mustard seed faith can move the mountain of
fear from my heart. Thank You, Lord.

April 16

*I smiled on them when they had no
confidence; and the light of my countenance they did not cast down.*

Job 29:24

Our Higher Power is aware of our
insecurities and fears. He is right here.
He smiles on me when I need him most.

Today, I come to Jesus Christ, and ask
Him into my heart. Fill me with Your love
and power. Guide me with Your spirit. In
You, Christ, I am free. No longer does fear
keep me a prisoner. In all situations, I am
free. My confidence is in You.

April 17

*Wait for the Lord; be strong, and let
your heart take courage.*

Psalm 27:14

Today, we will wait for the Lord.
Sometimes our fears have clouded our
lives and actions, but we must never give

up. We must be patient in changing the patterns we've held for so long.

Today, I will practice a simple faith, to live one day at a time, to have faith and patience.

As long as I follow Jesus, my Higher Power, I know that my recovery will continue. He will not leave me halfway through. I will courageously grow more and more into His likeness.

April 18

I am the Alpha and the Omega, the beginning and the end. To the thirsty I will give from the fountain of the water of life without payment.

Revelation 21:6

We in Phobics Victorious come to our Higher Power, Jesus. We surrender to Him asking Him to fill our thirsty, fearful souls with the water of life.

Jesus gives us this life as a free gift. He heals us and transforms us.

Holy Spirit, come into my heart today. Perform spiritual surgery on me. Give me a new life of faith and love and joy.

As one whom his mother comforts, so I will comfort you.

Isaiah 66:13

Our devastating panic attacks left us badly shaken. Our resulting actions hurt us. They deprived us of peace and joy. We, above all people, needed comfort.

I am thankful today that my Higher Power, Jesus, comforts me. In Him is my faith. I do not fear people nor places, nor things. I have all strength through Christ. He comforts me, making me feel safe. I will rest in You, today, Lord Jesus.

April 20

Live as free men, yet without using your freedom as a pretext for evil; but live as servants of God.

1 Peter2:16

As we emerge from our prisons, breaking free of our debilitating fears and addictions, let us remember to do what is right. Let us be kind and compassionate, forgiving of others and ourselves. Let us be pure and holy and temperate, for we are new creations in Christ. He dwells in us. We are being sanctified each day to reflect Him and to reveal His glory.

I will serve You today, dear God, by carrying the good news of the Twelve Steps of Phobics Victorious to others who are suffering and in need.

April 21

I will restore health to you.
Jeremiah 30:17

We know how devastating phobias and panic attacks are to our mental, emotional and even physical health. But we also know that our Higher Power, Jesus, has promised to restore health to us.

Today, I choose to think healthy thoughts. I choose to make healthy choices. I allow the Spirit of my Higher Power to work in me, making me healthy, whole, and free.

April 22

And the effect of righteousness will be peace, and the result of righteousness, guilt-lessness and trust forever.

Isaiah 32:17

In Phobics Victorious, we take a fourth

step inventory. This inventory is thorough and fearless. We try to get honest with ourselves. When we do this, we see areas of our lives where we have compromised moral or ethical values.

Today, I will be aware that as I become more honest and brave enough to clear out the garbage of my past, I will find fewer things to be afraid of. I will feel right with God and myself, I will have peace. I will quietly trust in my Higher Power, and His desire for good in my life.

April 23

Therefore we will not fear though the earth should change.

Psalm 46:2

In Phobics Victorious, we see beyond the physical realm. We grow spiritually as we become aware of a reality greater than our finite senses have known.

Because we know that our Higher Power lives, we are not afraid. The earth itself will be sanctified as we have been. Today, I commit my life again to Jesus, my Higher Power. I am not alone on this road of recovery.

Put a new and right spirit within me.
Psalm 51:10

The spirit of fear has held we phobics in a bondage that is not from God. We have chosen to recover from this; we are willing to turn our will and life over to God's care. He will put His spirit in all who come to Him.

Let me remember today that His Spirit is a gift to me. All power and authority is given to Jesus! His presence in me dispels all old fearful thoughts and behaviors. Today, I walk with a new and right spirit within me. Today, I trust in Him.

According to the riches of his glory, he may grant you to be strengthened with might through his Spirit in the inner man.
Ephesians 3:16

Phobic fears and panic attacks have truly weakened us. They are a weapon of the enemy. But, today I have a spiritual weapon. I am victorious over the enemy through Jesus Christ. His Spirit strengthens me.

I will walk today, strong and unafraid. I will have courage and be victorious for I am not alone. I do all things through my Higher Power, Jesus Christ.

April 26

Be transformed by the renewal of your mind, that you may prove what is the will of God, what is good and acceptable and perfect.

Romans 12:2

God is good. God is love. He created me in His image. He loves me. For phobics, fear has separated us from the love of God.

Today, I am being transformed from a consciousness of fear to a consciousness of love, faith and trust. God's will for me is good. As I allow Him to work His will in me, I become more tranquil and in harmony with God and others. I avoid fearful thoughts, doubts and despairs. I look up to Jesus. I cast my burdens on Him.

Be renewed in the spirit of your minds, and put on the new nature.

> Ephesians 4:23,24

The spirit of fear is not from God. We phobics have been in bondage, but we no longer need be slaves to fear.

Today, I put on the new nature of my Higher Power, Jesus. My mind is renewed. I am set free from fear. I walk by faith; I act in the power and strength of His might. Thank You, Jesus!

April 28

Be still and know that I am God.

> Psalm 46:10

We have often acted in either a frenzied state, or we have been immobilized and paralyzed by fear. Both conditions keep us from a knowledge of, and relationship with, our Higher Power, Jesus.

Today, I will still my mind and my body. I will be open and receptive to the Spirit of God. He will guide me into all truth, as I journey from darkness into light.

I lift up my eyes to the hills; From whence does my help come? My help comes from the Lord, who made heaven and earth.

Psalm 121 :1,2

We phobics have gone to many sources of help: doctors, medication, therapy. Sometimes these sources have helped, but we must realize the ultimate source of help is from God. Our Higher Power, Jesus, is the great Physician, the great Healer.

Having exhausted all other resources, I lift my eyes to You, Jesus. Please help me. Release me from the bondage of fear, from the bondage of self. Let me walk by faith not by sight.

The exceeding greatness of His power to usward who believe, according to the working of His mighty power.

Ephesians 1:19

Our Higher Power, Jesus Christ, is mighty. He is able to heal our disease, to cast out demons, to forgive our sins, to give us new life.

Today, I thank You, Jesus, for delivering me from the soul-sickness of fear. I give praise to Your name. I rejoice in You. I walk in resurrection power and victory.

May 1

Even the youths shall faint and be weary, and the young men utterly fall: but they that wait upon the Lord shall renew their strength; they shall mount up with wings as eagles; they shall run, and not be weary; and they shall walk and not faint.
Isaiah 40:30,31

We phobics have received a brutal battering by fear. On our own, we could not defeat it. But today, we give thanks to Jesus, who has overcome the world. Through faith in Him, we have victory over fear.

I will not be afraid, but will trust in Jesus in every circumstance. He will renew my strength. He will help me walk, run and even soar through life victoriously. Thank You, Jesus! Thank You, Lord! Hallelujah!

Thou shalt be steadfast, and shalt not fear: because thou shalt forget thy misery, and remember it as waters that pass away.
Job 11:15,16

As we phobics, who were bound by fear for so long, are now delivered from its grip, let us learn to walk in freedom; let us be steadfast.

When I fall into fearful thinking, full of doubts and confusion, I will call upon Jesus. I will ask Him for greater strength and faith. I will ask Him for a fuller understanding of God's love and His mighty power. I am assured that all memories of my misery will disappear.

May 3

Whoso putteth his trust in the Lord shall be safe.

Proverbs 29:25

Our adversary, the devil, uses fear to keep us from God and each other. Because of fear, relationships are destroyed. Countries fight. Religions disagree.

When we are afraid, let us put our trust in Jesus, our Higher Power. He will keep us safe. Today, I will remember that Jesus commands us to love one another. He asks us to forgive our enemies, to be merciful. When I am angry and fearful, I will think of Jesus.

May 4

Nor trust in uncertain riches, but in the living God, who giveth us richly all things to enjoy.

1 Timothy 6:17

Many of we phobics have feared economic insecurity. We have trusted material things or money to see us through. But Phobics Victorious is a spiritual program; we look to the Holy Spirit to lead us into truth.

Today I have faith that all my needs are being met by my Higher Power, Jesus Christ. He tells us not to worry about what we will eat or drink. We are to seek Him first. He will provide everything we need. He gives us life.

The Lord is nigh unto all them that call upon Him, to all that call upon Him in truth.
Psalm 145:18

Thank You, Jesus, for being right here with me. I need not be afraid of anything. Your life and power within me will keep me today.

Today, I reflect on Jesus. I ask His Holy Spirit to fill me and guide me. I will feel His loving, comforting presence wherever I go. In Him, I am safe, and I am never alone.

And every man that hath this hope in him purifieth himself, even as He is pure.
1 John 3:3

As we journey from the darkness of fear and depression into the light of His love, we see many unclean areas of our lives. We desire to be clean, to be holy, to be pure. We cannot accomplish this alone, nor overnight.

Today, dear Lord, please sanctify some part of me. Lead me not into temptation. Deliver me from evil. Create in me a clean heart. Renew my mind. Thank You, Jesus.

In returning and rest shall ye be saved; in quietness and in confidence shall be your strength.

Isaiah 30:15

We have found that trying to deal with fear our own way, the way of the world, is unsuccessful. We had to surrender to our Higher Power, Jesus. We turned over our lives and wills. Our salvation began here. We could rest in Him, and allow His spirit to set us free.

Today, I am quietly confident in my Higher Power. In Him, I can do all things. He is my strength. I will quietly, confidently rest in His love.

I am with thee to deliver thee.

Jeremiah 1:8

The horror of phobias and panic attacks is too terrible to describe fully. This affliction destroys the joy of life. It holds us in utter bondage.

My prayer today, Lord Jesus, is to be

totally delivered from destructive fear. Allow me to walk in the light of life, full of love and power. Let my life glorify You. Let me follow You.

May 9

Cast thy burden upon the Lord, and He shall sustain thee; He shall never suffer the righteous to be moved.
Psalm 55:22

As we walk a spiritual path to recovery, by following Jesus and the Twelve Step program, we sometimes meet obstacles. We are often assaulted by worldly concerns. Sometimes we are persecuted. We may relapse into negative, fearful thinking and behavior patterns.

Today, I look anew to my Higher Power, Jesus. Whatever circumstances I face, I know He is with me. He will carry my burden and keep me safe. As long as I follow Him, I need not fall back into despair. He will hold me steady and strong. He has already overcome the world.

*Be merciful unto me, 0 God, be merciful
unto me: for my soul trusteth in thee: yea,
in the shadow of thy wings will I make my
refuge, until these calamities be overpast.*

Psalm 57:1

Because of irrational fears, we phobics
have found ourselves in a tangle of self-
defeating behavior patterns. Instead of
walking by faith, we've walked by fear.

Today, I will trust in my Higher Power,
Jesus. He provides a refuge for my soul.
He will keep me safe until crises pass.
In His mercy, He will bring me through
trials and tribulations. He will transform
my life. In Him, I am an overcomer of
destructive fear.

*The Lord bless thee, and keep thee:
the Lord make His face shine upon thee,
and be gracious unto thee: the Lord lift up
His countenance upon thee, and give thee
peace.*

Numbers 6:24-26

We phobics' lives have been riddled with
anxieties. It was not until we surrendered

our wills and our lives to our Higher Power, Jesus Christ, that we began to know peace.

Today, as I walk with Jesus, I am full of His peace. God's grace sets me free from doubt, confusion and fear. I have the mind of Christ. In all my affairs, I am gracious. I realize the flesh profited nothing. It is the spirit that is eternal.

May 12

He giveth His beloved sleep.
Psalm 127:2

Panic attacks and anxiety often interrupt peaceful sleep. Many phobics awake suddenly in the night, gripped with terror and panic.

Today, I will know that as I walk with Him and invite His Spirit to dwell in me, I will be at peace — safe in the protective arms of my Heavenly Father, of the Lord Jesus Christ, and of His Holy Spirit. I will be calm and serene, free from panic, both awake and asleep.

Who hearkeneth unto me shall dwell safely, and shall be quiet from fear of evil.
Proverbs 1:33

Phobics receive welcome news in this scripture! We fear abandonment, economic insecurity, people, places and things. All of life becomes terrifying. One really cannot call this life. It's more like being in a prison.

But Jesus, our Higher Power, sets us free. My prayer today is to improve my conscious contact with Jesus. I will seek to know His will and to receive the power to carry it out.

We know that all things work together for good to them that love God.
Romans 8:28

Sometimes our phobias and panic attacks have so adversely affected our lives, that we lose sight of God's love and power. We forget that God is good, that He sees the bigger picture. As long as we follow Him, He is faithful and just to bring us good.

Today, I reflect on God's love for me. I worship Him, and I praise His name. I am thankful that He has redeemed me, that He is my Savior. I look forward to seeing how He brings good out of my painful past.

May 15

I waited patiently for the Lord; and He inclined unto me, and heard my cry.
Psalm 40:1

Sometimes it seems as if our phobias and panic attacks will never leave us. Some of us have given up hope; we have even despaired of our lives. For some, death seemed better than a life of fear.

But, today, I will accept the life that You offer me. It is a free gift. This is resurrection life — free, full of power, full of love. Thank You, Jesus, for hearing my cry and changing my direction from devastation to joy.

May 16

Bear ye one another's burdens, and so fulfill the law of Christ.
Galatians 6:2

In our recovery from phobias and panic attacks, we've found that as we receive help, we also need to give help. This is not a self-serving program. As we focus on Jesus, we realize that it is in giving that we receive.

Today, I will practice the twelfth step, to carry the message to others. I will be compassionate, kind, and caring to suffering phobics. I will remember how I once suffered, and will try to lighten the load of fellow phobics.

May 17

Great peace have they which love Thy law: and nothing shall offend them.
Psalm 119:165

Sin brings anxiety and separates us from God. In our fourth step, personal and fearless moral inventory, we examine ourselves for defects of character. We clean house.

Lord Jesus, I know I am sometimes blind to my own faults. I cannot clearly see myself. Fill me with Your Spirit that I might see my errors and correct them. Sanctify me and give me strength to do Your will.

He healeth the broken in heart, and bindeth up their wounds. He telleth the number of the stars; He calleth them all by their names.

Psalm 147:3-4

Phobias and panic attacks are part of a broken person. We know we're not functioning in a sound and healthy manner. We feel much grief and shame.

Today, I turn to my Higher Power, Jesus. He heals my diseases. He restores health and wholeness to me. He gives me a new heart and renews my mind. I am a new person in Christ. Thank You, Jesus!

My presence shall go with thee, and I will give thee rest.

Exodus 33:14

It has been utterly exhausting, physically, emotionally, mentally, and spiritually, to fight our irrational fears by ourselves.

Today, I surrender to my Higher Power, Jesus Christ. I cast my burdens on Him. I turn over my anxieties to Him.

He will not leave me, nor forsake me. I rest in His presence.

May 20

Finally, my brethren, be strong in the Lord, and in the power of His might.
Ephesians 6:10

Let us not take back our anxieties once we have cast them on our Lord. Let us walk by faith in His power and His strength to heal our lives.

Today, I know that our Higher Power, Jesus, is mighty. He has overcome disease, death and the world. In Him, I claim complete victory, as I live in His resurrection power.

May 21

To be spiritually minded is life and peace.
Romans 8:6

When we become spiritually minded, we begin to change our perspective. We view our lives as part of a bigger picture. We rest assured that in God's own time and space, according to divine order, all things work for good. All we need to do is follow Him each day.

Today, I will not follow my own way, for that has not always led me into happiness. I will follow His way. In Him, there is no fear.

May 22

In the day when I cried Thou answered me, and strengthenest me with strength in my soul.

Psalm 138:3

We phobics tried so hard to hang on to our own ways and devices. Yet, they didn't work. We found that in yielding control of our lives to God, He strengthened our weaknesses. We became strong in our souls.

Today, I come again to Jesus. I cast my cares on Him. He gives me strength in all I do; and I am no longer afraid.

May 23

I have blotted out, as a thick cloud, thy transgressions, and, as a cloud, thy sins: return unto me; for I have redeemed thee.

Isaiah 44:22

Our defects of character, the soul-sickness of fear, have led us into many life destroying patterns. When we come to our Higher Power, Jesus, we leave all these defects at the cross. He has already paid the price. We are redeemed.

Thank You, Jesus, for saving me from my sins, from my self-willed way. Thank You for giving me new life, based on faith, not fear. I am redeemed by the blood of the lamb. I am cleansed from all sin.

May 24

What time I am afraid, I will trust in Thee.

Psalm 56:3

When I fall back into fear, doubt and confusion, I will go to the foot of the cross. I will lay these burdens there.

Because my Higher Power, Jesus, is mighty, victorious and powerful, I will simply trust in Him. When I am afraid, I will focus on Jesus, who calmed the storm, walked on water, healed the sick, cast out demons, made the blind to see and rose from the dead. In Him I am set free.

Fearfulness and trembling are come upon me, and horror hath overwhelmed me. And I said, Oh that I had wings like a dove! For then would I fly away, and be at rest.

Psalm 55:5-6

Fear destroys. Love builds. As long as we phobics choose to live by fear, our lives will be adversely affected. We must admit that even if we flew to some distant land, we would take our fear with us. It is part of us. Let us choose to live by faith. We already know we cannot accomplish this alone.

Today, I come to my Higher Power, Jesus. In Him I rest By His power and might, I am free from fear. Through His love, I am not afraid.

Create in me a clean heart, 0 God; and renew a right spirit within me. Cast me not away from thy presence: and take not thy Holy Spirit from me.

Psalm 51:10-11

Because we phobics have been so afraid,

we've allowed doubt, confusion and despair to rule in our lives. We need to break these destructive patterns of living.

Through my Higher Power, Jesus Christ, and His Holy Spirit dwelling in me, I am a new person. The Holy Spirit cleanses my heart. Old negative, fearful ways are gone. I have a new, clean heart full of love.

May 27

He brought me up also out of an horrible pit, out of the miry clay and set my feet upon a rock, and established my goings.

Psalm 40:2

Fears, phobias and panic attacks are definitely a horrible pit. They have led to unhealthy and ungodly behavior patterns. We came to realize we could not get out of this pit by ourselves.

Jesus, thank You for bringing me out of that horrible pit. Thank You for delivering me from evil. Thank You for saving me. Let my walk be on firm footing from now on. You are my Rock. Establish my life on You.

The Lord is my rock, and my fortress, and my deliverer, my God, my strength, in whom I will trust.

Psalm 18:2

We phobics have tried so many ways to deal with our fears. We avoided people or places or things. We often used alcohol or drugs to self medicate. We hoarded material things for security. We acted compulsively and impulsively. When all this did not work, we came to our Higher Power.

Our Higher Power, Jesus, is my rock. He stabilizes me. I trust in Him. He tells me, "Be not afraid." Today, I will walk on solid ground, confident and serene.

How long wilt thou forget me, 0 Lord ? forever? How long wilt thou hide thy face from me? How long shall I take counsel in my soul, having sorrow in my heart daily?

Psalm 13:1-2

The above scripture is the cry of many phobics who are in bondage to fear. Because of fear, we have failed to feel the presence of God and His great love for us.

Today, I will increase my faith in God. I am His child. He is my Heavenly Father. He loves me and desires to fellowship with me. Through my faith and belief in Him, I am healthy, whole, and free.

May 30

Have mercy upon me, 0 Lord; for I am weak: 0 Lord, heal me; for my bones are vexed.

Psalm 6:2

Sometimes we phobics feel so weak, so helpless to handle our irrational fears. It is then that we surrender them to our Higher Power, Jesus Christ. He tells us to bring our burdens to Him and leave them there.

Today, I will examine the life of Jesus Christ. He listened to people's hurts and healed them. In Him is power over all aspects of nature, over disease, over demons, and over death. He tells me, "Lo I am with You always."

Behold, God is my salvation, I will trust, and not be afraid; for the Lord Jehovah is my strength and my song; He also is become my salvation.

Isaiah 12:2

We phobics desire, more than anything, to be saved from fear. We know we can not do that on our own.

Today, I will turn to my Higher Power, Jesus Christ. He is my strength; He is my song. I trust in Him. Jesus is my salvation. I am not afraid.

Stand fast therefore in the liberty wherewith Christ has made us free, and be not entangled again with the yoke of bondage.

Galatians 5:1

Phobias and panic attacks are a form of bondage. But we in Phobics Victorious have freedom in Jesus Christ.

Today, I walk in freedom from phobias and panic attacks. I will take my daily inventory and try to be right with God. Anything that disturbs my serenity, I will detach from. Today, I choose liberty from past behaviors.

June 2

Wait on the Lord: be of good courage, and He shall strengthen thine heart: wait, I say, on the Lord.

Psalm 27:14

We have come to Jesus with our irrational fears. We have laid them at the foot of the cross. Jesus is our Great Physician, our Counselor, I cast my burdens on Him.

I will courageously face today, for Jesus, my Higher Power, has redeemed me. I am not alone. I will be patient knowing that He is transforming my life.

June 3

He giveth power to the faint; and to them that have no might He increaseth strength.

Isaiah 40:29

On our own, we phobics were powerless over fear. We had to get to the end of ourselves, before we looked to Jesus our Higher Power. He is the Savior of our souls.

Thank You, Jesus, for saving me. Thank You for giving me strength when I had none. Thank You for empowering my life. Help me to be mindful of You.

June 4

We then that are strong ought to bear the infirmities of the weak, and not to please ourselves.

Romans 15:1

We are set free to serve. Phobics Victorious uses our victory over fear to help other suffering phobics. We practice the Twelfth Step to carry the message to others.

Today, I will carry the message of the Twelfth Step; in doing that, I am also sharing the Good News of the Gospel of Jesus Christ. I no longer live to please myself, but to please Him.

June 5

Being confident of this very thing, that He which hath begun a good work in you will perform it.

Philippians 1:6

We find in the Holy Scriptures many references to fear. We are told to fear the

Lord, but to " be not afraid. " Walking in the fear of the Lord is to respect Him and to obey His commandments. To be not afraid is to trust in Him and have faith that He is faithful, just, good, and loving.

I will not regress in my walk of faith by taking back control of my life. I surrender my will and life anew today to Jesus Christ. He will perform good things for me.

June 6

What time I am afraid, I will trust in Thee.
Psalm 56:3

Phobias are irrational fears. They seem uncontrollable. They are not of the Lord. In my own strength, I cannot resist them.

Today, I will resist phobias and panic attacks through the power and authority of Jesus Christ. It is in His might and strength that I have victory. He gives me the peace of God, which surpasses all understanding.

0 Lord, I am oppressed; undertake for me.
Isaiah 38:14

Phobias, panic attacks and often accompanying depression are all forms of oppression.

Oh, Lord, today I pray for ministering angels to encamp around me. I pray for protection and freedom from fear and depression. I know I am redeemed by the blood of the Lamb. Evil cannot touch me when I am covered with Christ's blood. I claim this now. I live in resurrection power. I walk in the power of the Holy Spirit. Hallelujah! I praise You Jesus! I glorify Your name!

June 8

When I awake, I am still with Thee.
Psalm 139:18

In the stillness of the early morning, I feel the presence of God. Nature testifies to me of His love and grace, that His mercies are new each morning.

Let me not rush into the day. Let me adopt the pace of nature. I will remember that there is a time and season for all

things. I will simply trust in Him. I will
be still and know that He is God.

June 9

*When I sit in darkness, the Lord shall
be a light unto me.*

Micah 7:8

Jesus is the light of the world. All
around us the world lies in darkness, but
Jesus shows us the way. His way is not
the world's way.

Today, I will be careful not to get
caught up in the world's way of rushing,
acquiring, troubling, fighting. I will
focus on Jesus. My trust will not be in
money or things or people, but in Him.
He has shown us His power and victory
over the world.

June 10

*I had fainted unless I had believed to
see the goodness of the Lord in the land of
the living.*

Psalm 27:13

The second step of Phobics Victorious
says, "We came to believe that a power
greater than ourselves could restore us

to sanity." Without this belief, we would have perished.

Today, I know that God is good. He is love. Perfect love does not have fear. Dear God, help me to love like You love. Fill me with Your love. I receive Your love today. Thank You, Jesus.

June 11

He that believeth shall not make haste.
Isaiah 28:16

When we know we have a Heavenly Father who created us and who loves us, we know that we are special.

I am a Child of God. He cares for me. I need not rush about trying to do things my way, trying to get what I want right now. Today, I will rest in Him. I will trust in Him. He sees the end from the beginning. I wait for Him. Thank You, Lord, for directing my path.

June 12

Now the Lord of peace Himself give you peace always by all means.
II Thessalonians 3:16

Being afflicted by phobias and panic

attacks leaves us in a tremendous state of anxiety. When we come to our Higher Power, Jesus, we cast our anxieties upon Him.

Today, Jesus fills me with His peace. All anxiety is gone, as I rest in Him. He renews a quiet spirit within me. I am peaceful and content. He says He will never leave me, nor forsake me.

June 13

The Lord is faithful, who shall establish you, and keep you from evil.
II Thessalonians 3:3

Irrational fears, phobias, and panic attacks have been an evil, which has destructively affected our lives. When we came to God in prayer, we asked Him to deliver us from evil.

I know that my Lord is a faithful Lord. He is also powerful. I ask my Heavenly Father, in the name of Jesus, to deliver me from evil. Establish me in Your will.

Behold, I have refined thee, but not with silver; I have chosen thee in the furnace of affliction.

Isaiah 48:10

Being afflicted with phobias and panic attacks is a terrible thing. But we in Phobics Victorious know there is a way out. That way is Jesus.

Today, I follow Jesus. I am being conformed into His image, day by day. I have gone through the phobic's furnace of afflictions, but He has purified me and delivered me now. I am purified in Christ.

And the Lord, He it is that doth go before thee, He will be with thee, He will not fail thee, neither forsake thee: fear not, neither be dismayed.

Deuteronomy 31:8

Phobias alienate us from people and places. Fear destroys our quality of life. But we turn to our Higher Power, Jesus Christ. All power and authority are given to Jesus.

I am not afraid. I have Jesus in my

heart. He will never leave me. In place of my old spirit of fear and dismay, I choose the gift of life, of love.

June 16

Now the God of hope fill you with all joy and peace in believing that ye may abound in hope, through the power of the Holy Ghost.

Romans 15:13

Our second step in Phobics Victorious is the belief step. We must come to believe that our Higher Power will restore us to sanity or wholeness. Our hope is in Jesus Christ.

Dear Jesus, please fill me today with Your joy and peace. Help me abound in hope. I choose to follow You, Jesus. You are the way, the truth and the life. I know I can do all things through You.

June 17

For the Lord shall be thy confidence.
Proverbs 3:26

In and of myself, I can do nothing. I desire to be free of phobias and depression. I cast these burdens on the Lord.

Today, I walk in total confidence, because I walk in Christ. I am peaceful and joyous. Jesus is with me. His Holy Spirit dwells in me. He sets me free.

June 18

Seek not ye what ye shall eat, or what ye shall drink, neither be ye of doubtful mind.
Luke 12:29

We recovering phobics must not give in to doubt. We need to increase our faith in our Higher Power. Our faith is in God and His son, Jesus Christ. All power and authority is given to Jesus. We can do all things through Him.

I believe in my Heavenly Father. He loves me. I believe in His Son, Jesus Christ. He is the Savior of my soul. I believe Jesus died for my sins and that He arose from the dead. He overcame all disease and death. I believe He is healing me now. Thank You, Jesus!

June 19

We which have believed do enter into rest.
Hebrews 4:3

We in Phobics Victorious don't need

to struggle with, nor fight, our phobias and panic attacks. We let go of our fears and let God take control. We come to Jesus, and He gives us rest.

Today, I will give all my fear, despair, doubt, confusion and depression to Jesus. I lay these weaknesses at the foot of the cross. I will not take them back. I lay them there, and I rest in His love and power.

June 20

Hast thou not known? Hast thou not heard, that the everlasting God, the Lord, the Creator of the ends of the earth, fainteth not, neither is weary? He giveth power to the faint, and to them that have no might He increaseth strength.

Isaiah 40:28-29

Fear has thrashed our lives. We've felt beaten up by irrational fears, doubts, and depressions. Trying to fight these on our own has led to total exhaustion. Our own self-will, our determination for control has not worked. Some of us have ravaged our bodies and minds with alcohol and drugs.

Today, I have confidence in the strength of my Higher Power, Jesus Christ. I am weary, 0 Lord. Please carry

me in Your arms. Touch me and heal me.
Fill me with new strength, joy, and energy. Thank You, Jesus.

June 21

The peace of God, which passeth all under-standing, shall keep your hearts and minds through Christ Jesus.
Philippians 4:7

Before we became victorious over our irrational fears through our Higher Power, Jesus Christ, we phobics lived in constant dread and anxiety. We avoided people, places and things that we were afraid of.

Today, in Phobics Victorious, I have the peace of God in my heart. Jesus has saved me from my sins. He has healed my soul-sickness. I am a new person in Christ: healthy, whole and free.

June 22

Let the peace of God rule in your hearts.
Colossians 3:15

Irrational fear and anxiety are destructive emotions. They rule over our lives like a tyrannical dictator. God wants His peace to rule in our hearts. When we sin or do not obey His commandments, we separate ourselves from His love and peace.

Today, I come to Jesus. I ask Him to fill me with His peace. I confess my sins, and I ask for divine guidance and power in walking in obedience. The blood of Jesus Christ cleanses me from all sin. He is the way, the truth, and life.

June 23

Forgetting those things which are behind, and reaching forth unto those things which are before, I press toward the mark for the prize of the high calling of God in Christ Jesus.

Philippians 3:13-14

We phobics have been torn apart by our fears and panic attacks. All areas of our lives were affected. Because of fear, confusion and doubt, we lost much.

Today, I let go of the past. I am a new person in Christ. I am growing up in Him. As a Child of God, I am growing spiritually. I will not look back. My faith and belief are increasing. God loves me and has given His spirit to me. He comforts me.

Delight thyself also in the Lord; and he shall give thee the desires of thine heart.
                              Psalm 37:4

As phobics, we used to run around, on our own, trying ways to alleviate our anxiety and insecurity. We tried alcohol, drugs, money, unhealthy relationships, seclusion, isolation, and aggression. Yet none of these ways gave us freedom. They often became prisons in and of themselves.

Today, in Phobics Victorious, I put my Higher Power, the Lord Jesus Christ, first. I choose to follow Him. He tells me to ask, and I will receive. This is a promise, which He will always keep.

June 25

In God have I put my trust; I will not be afraid what man can do unto me.
                              Psalm 56:11

In Phobics Victorious, we walk by faith. We resist fear. We surrender our will and life to our Higher Power, Jesus Christ. With Him in charge, we need not be afraid.

Today, I praise the name of Jesus. He

is mighty and powerful. Jesus has all power over disease, demons, nature, and death. Yet He is loving, kind, forgiving, compassionate, and merciful. He teaches us sacrificial service. He commands us to, "Love one another, as I have loved You."

June 26

If any of you lack wisdom, let him ask of God, that giveth to all men liberally, and upbraideth not, and it shall be given him. But let him ask in faith, nothing wavering. For he that wavereth is like a wave of the sea, driven with the wind and tossed.

James 1:5-6

We phobics have had our thoughts clouded by fear and anxiety. We've let doubt and despair steer us off course. We lacked faith to persevere, to endure. We felt unwise and unsure about our decisions.

But today, I have victory in Jesus. With my eyes fixed on Him, I walk by faith. I know He loves me. He is my friend. He desires to give me wisdom and joy. I accept You, Jesus. I accept Your gift of stability and strength.

God resisteth the proud, but giveth grace unto the humble.

James 4:6

As long as we phobics think we know all the answers, or that we can recover on our own resources, we block the power of our Creator God. God does not want us in rebellion to Him.

Today, I humble myself before my Almighty Father. I conform my will to His will. I receive His love. I choose to obey Him and know I cannot do this on my own. I need His Spirit and His grace. Thank You, Heavenly Father.

June 28

Submit yourselves therefore to God. Resist the devil, and he will flee from you.

James 4:7

We have been so afraid that we would not get what we wanted. Because of our phobias and insecurities, we fell into the trap of the devil's lies. We did not submit ourselves to God.

Today, I know that God desires good things for my life. God is good! God desires to fill me with His Spirit. God is all powerful! God loves me and offers me His love. God is love! I receive Your love, today, Lord. When fear and doubt and depression seek to turn me away from God, I resist them. I submit to You, instead.

June 29

Humble yourself in the sight of the Lord, and he shall lift you up.

James 4:10

It is in giving that we receive. It is in surrendering control that we get back control of our lives. It is in becoming humble that we are lifted up.

Today, dear Higher Power, I acknowledge my total need for You. I submit to Your Lordship, dear Jesus. I turn my will and life over to You. I believe You love me, that You died for my sins. I praise You and thank You, my Redeemer, my Savior.

Confess your faults one to another, and pray one for another, that ye may be healed. The effectual fervent prayer of a righteous man availeth much.

James 5:16

We in Phobics Victorious have been afflicted with a grave disorder. Panic disorder interferes with all areas of life. It's negative impact is devastating.

Today, I know I can have victory over fear. I do not allow fear to disrupt my life. I challenge the spirit of fear in the name of Jesus Christ. Through the power and authority of Jesus, I cast out fear. I pray for the Holy Spirit to fill me. I am free.

For so is the will of God, that with well doing ye may put to silence the ignorance of foolish men: As free, and not using your liberty for a cloak of maliciousness, but as the servants of God.

1 Peter 2:15-16

We in Phobics Victorious are free. Learning to walk in freedom and liberty is a process. We need to always be dependent on our Higher Power, Jesus Christ. We conform our will to the will of our Heavenly Father.

Lord Jesus, You have set us free to serve. Let me love and serve in meekness of spirit. Let me never forget, that except for the grace of God, I would still be in bondage. Thank You, Jesus.

July 2

And who is he that will harm you, if ye be followers of that which is good? But, and if ye suffer for righteousness sake, happy are ye; and be not afraid of their terror, neither be troubled.

1 Peter 3:13-14

Fear breeds a ground of violence and destruction. Because of fear, people accuse each other. Fear severs relationships.

I will not give in to fear. When it strikes, I resist it. I choose to follow Jesus. In Him, I am free. In my place with Christ, I have power and authority over fear. My only goal is to follow Jesus, the way, the truth and the life. He tells me, "Be not afraid."

Be sober, be vigilant; because your ad-versary the devil, as a roaring lion, walketh about seeking whom he may devour.

1 Peter 5:8

Many of us phobics tried to drown our fears in alcohol and drugs. Taken to excess, this left us in a drunken state. We were not clearheaded. By clouding our perceptions, we gave the devil opportunity to gain a foothold in our lives.

Today, I choose to walk in light and truth. I choose to see clearly, to take part in life. It is only through the spirit of God in me that I am able to do this. Come, Holy Spirit, come in; I welcome You into my life.

But the God of all grace, who hath called us into his eternal glory by Christ Jesus, after that ye have suffered a while, make you perfect, establish, strengthen, settle you.

1 Peter 5:10

Phobias and panic attacks and our subsequent behaviors brought much suffering into our lives. We were terribly oppressed by fear.

But as we continue our spiritual recovery, we begin to realize that fear is a lie, a false belief that distorts reality; it clouds our perception of God, life, love, beauty and truth. Today, I stand firm and trust in Jesus to perfect my weaknesses, stabilize my walk and settle me in Him.

July 5

While they promise them liberty, they themselves are the servants of corruption: for of whom a man is overcome, of the same is he brought in bondage.

II Peter 2:19

When we let fears, phobias and panic attacks control our life, and believe in their destructive lies, we live under bondage. When we use alcohol and drugs, thinking they will give us freedom, we become in bondage to them.

Our freedom is in Jesus Christ. He is the way, the truth and the life. As we know the truth, we are set free. Today, I keep my focus on Jesus. I cling to the cross. I remember that where His Spirit is, there is freedom.

If we confess our sins, he is faithful and just to forgive us our sins, and to cleanse us from all unrighteousness.

1 John 1 :9

Sin separates us from the presence of God. But God loves us so much. Through our Lord and Savior, Jesus Christ, we are reconciled to God the Father. We are redeemed. Jesus has taken all our sins upon Him, and through His blood we are cleansed.

Today, I will do my daily personal inventory.

Where I find that I've let sin separate me from God, I will quickly confess it. I am open to His sanctifying work in me. I am willing to be conformed to His image. Jesus was not afraid. He is victorious, and He dwells in me!

Greater is he that is in you, than he that is in the world.

1 John 4:4

We recovering phobics know that God did not give us a spirit of fear. We also know that Satan is the father of lies. He deceives us about our true nature.

In Phobics Victorious, we are not alone. We have our Higher Power, Jesus Christ, dwelling in us. As we abide in Him, we are one with God the Father, His son Jesus, and the Holy Spirit. Doubt, confusion, fear, and panic fall into insignificance in the presence of our Higher Power.

July 8

There is no fear in love; but perfect love casteth out fear: because fear hath torment. He that feareth is not made perfect in love.

1 John 4:18

Fear is a great destroyer of relationships. It gives a foothold to doubt, negative thinking, distrust, lack of belief and lack of faith.

We in Phobics Victorious must avoid negative fearful thinking and beliefs. We are to take those thoughts captive to stop them. Today, I will immediately shift my focus to God, to His goodness, His divine justice and His outworking in my life. I will focus on Jesus and His love for me, and His victory over darkness. Lord, I receive a fresh infilling of Your love in me today.

July 9

No man hath seen God at anytime. If we love one another, God dwelleth in us, and his love is perfected in us.

1 John 4:12

We know that fear interferes with our ability to give and receive love. Without love, we die. Love is a choice, and today I choose love.

I know that Jesus, my Higher Power, loves me and that His spirit of love dwells in me. I have faith in the love of God. He will perfect His love in me.

July 10

He that loveth not knoweth not God; for God is love.

1 John 4:8

We phobics had been too afraid to love fully and freely. We lacked faith in our Higher Power and in ourselves. Our trust in God, in ourselves and in others became undermined by fear. Fear was indeed our deadly enemy.

But, today, I walk by faith. My trust is in God. He loves me. He is all powerful. Fear is a defeated foe. God is good and just. He knows the beginning and the end. His divine blueprint of good, love, beauty, joy, peace, and righteousness is mine, if I but choose to follow Him and surrender to His will.

July 11

Herein is our love made perfect, that we may have boldness in the day of judgment: because as he is, so are we in this world.

1 John 4:17

We phobics know that boldness was not one of our attributes. We were either too fearful and self-conscious to even speak or act, or we aggressively pushed our way through.

Today, I have the love of God in me. I am in a firm place. My feet are on a rock. I go boldly forth in the knowledge of who I am, a beloved child of God.

By this we know that we love the children of God, when we love God, and keep his commandments.

1 John 5:2

As recovering phobics, we found that when we tried to do things "our way" we remained anxious and fearful. Our freedom from fear rested on us resting on God. We had to fully surrender our will and our life over to the care of our Higher Power.

Today, I have a loving relationship with my Higher Power, Jesus Christ. I am growing closer to Him each day and understanding His love for me. As I grow spiritually, my love for Him grows, and I desire to keep His commandments.

For whatsoever is born of God overcometh the world: and this is the victory that overcometh the world, even our faith.

1 John 5:4

In Phobics Victorious, we overcame fear through faith in our Higher Power,

Jesus Christ. His Spirit dwells in us. Where His Spirit is, there is freedom.

Today, I walk by faith. I focus on Jesus. In Him, I have complete victory over fear, disease, and death. Thank You, Jesus, for delivering me. Jesus is my Savior. I give Him praise!

July 14

Little children, keep yourselves from idols.
1 John 5:21

In Phobics Victorious, we put God first. We put our faith and trust in God, the Father, in His son, Jesus Christ, and in His Holy Spirit. These three are one, our Higher Power. Our attention and focus stay on our Higher Power. When we become unduly preoccupied with the cares or pleasures of this world, we shift our focus back onto Jesus.

Today, I will not let idols control or direct my life. Money, material pursuits, people, power, addictions to alcohol, drugs, food, exercise, gambling, sex, or to anything, will not take God's place in my life.

*Fear not; I am the first and the last:
I am he that liveth, and was dead; and
behold, I am alive for evermore, Amen;
and have the keys of hell and of death.*

Revelation 1:17-18

In Phobics Victorious, our Higher Power, Jesus Christ, tells us to fear not. He has overcome this world.

Thank You, Jesus, for coming to this world to show us the way and to save us. I accept You as my Lord and Savior. I invite You into my heart and life. From today forward I will follow You and live in resurrection power. I am a new creation in Christ.

*He that overcometh, the same shall
be clothed in white raiment; and I will
not blot out his name out of the book of
life, but I will confess his name before my
Father, and before his angels.*

Revelation 3:5

In Phobics Victorious, we are overcomers. We have overcome fear, disease and death. Our faith is in Jesus Christ, the way, the truth and the life.

Today, I confess the name of Jesus before men. I know that as I confess His name, He confesses me to God the Father. The blood of Jesus cleanses me from all sin. Though my sins were as scarlet, they are now white as snow. Thank You, Jesus! You are King of kings and Lord of lords.

July 17

Behold, I stand at the door, and knock; if any man hear my voice, and open the door, I will come in to him, and will sup with him, and he with me.

Revelation 3:20

As recovering phobics, we could not battle the enemy, fear, on our own strength. We were powerless over it. We were beaten down, almost destroyed.

Jesus stands at the door. I open my heart to You, Jesus, and I invite You in to dwell with me. You tell me to fear not. Through Your power and strength, I am an overcomer. I love You, Jesus, and I commit my life to You.

They shall hunger no more, neither thirst any more; neither shall the sun light on them, nor any heat. For the Lamb which is in the midst of the throne shall feed them, and shall lead them unto living fountains of waters. And God shall wipe away all tears from their eyes.

Revelation 7:16-17

In Phobics Victorious, our hope is in Jesus Christ! All the pain and fear and suffering will be gone. When Jesus returns, He will establish His kingdom of love, beauty, joy and peace. He will wipe away all our tears.

Today, Lord Jesus, I am walking in Your Kingdom. Your kingdom is within me. I know that in my spiritual journey, I will grow from glory to glory. Through the sanctification process, I am being conformed to the image of God.

I am Alpha and Omega, the beginning and the end, the first and the last.

Revelation 22:13

All power in Heaven and Earth is given to Jesus. In Phobics Victorious, let us continually look to Jesus. He is the way, the truth, and the life. In Him is complete victory over fear.

I rest in You, Lord Jesus, and in the power of your might. You are mighty God, the everlasting Father, the Prince of Peace. You have given us Your Holy Spirit, the Comforter, who guides us into all truth. We praise You and worship You!

July 20

Therefore, my beloved brethren, be ye steadfast, unmovable, always abounding in the work of the Lord, for as much as ye know that your labour is not in vain in the Lord.

1 Corinthians 15:58

In Phobics Victorious, Jesus is our rock. We follow Him. We do not turn back.

Today, as I carry the message of Jesus Christ in Phobics Victorious, I know that my labor is not in vain. He will never leave me nor forsake me. The twelfth step of Phobics Victorious tells me to carry the message to suffering phobics, and I will.

Blessed be God, even the Father of our Lord Jesus Christ, the Father of mercies, and the God of all comfort; Who comforteth us in all our tribulation, that we may be able to comfort them which are in any trouble, by the comfort wherewith we ourselves are comforted of God.

II Corinthians 1:3-4

As recovering phobics in Christ, we have mercy on others. We know what it feels like to suffer. We know what mistakes and sinful behaviors we adopted to deal with fear. But Jesus was merciful to us, so we are merciful to others.

Today, I will be merciful to others. They may have hurt me badly, because of their own fears and insecurities. I forgive them, Lord Jesus, as You forgave me. I pray for them, that they may know You.

And God is able to make all grace abound toward you; that ye, always having all sufficiency in all things may abound to every good work.

II Corinthians 9:8

Thank You, Lord Jesus, our Higher Power, for bestowing Your grace on Phobics Victorious. We didn't deserve it. We can't pay enough to earn it. We commit Phobics Victorious to You, to glorify Your name. We give You praise and thanksgiving. Your love dwells in our hearts.

Today, through the grace of God, I am an overcomer. I want to abound in good works. I walk in faith, not fear. I walk in love and peace.

I receive Your joy, my Lord. Thank You, Jesus.

July 23

For the weapons of our warfare are not carnal, but mighty through God to the pulling down of strong holds.
II Corinthians 10:4

Fear and depression have been strongholds in the lives of phobics. We found that we needed spiritual weapons to achieve victory in our battle.

Today, in the name of Jesus Christ, I command any spirit of fear or depression to leave me and to go to a place where Jesus sends you. I am free. Thank You, Jesus.

My grace is sufficient for thee: for my strength is made perfect in weakness.
                                    II Corinthians 12:9

On our own without our Higher Power, we phobics are powerless. But through the strength and power of Jesus Christ, we are victorious.

Today, I rest in Jesus. His grace is sufficient for me. Out of my weakness, He brings His strength. Without Him I can do nothing. With Him, I have life abundant and bear much fruit.

Examine yourselves, whether ye be in the faith: prove your own selves. Know ye not your own selves, how that Jesus Christ is in you, except ye be reprobate.
                                    II Corinthians 13:5

In Phobics Victorious, we take our fourth step: a personal and fearless moral inventory. We look in the mirror and get honest.

Today, I am willing to break through all denial, self deception, and delusion; I will thoroughly "clean my house." When

I say 'clean my house,' I mean I will face and clean up areas where I harbor rationalized sin. I ask for Your grace and strength, Lord Jesus. I ask my Heavenly Father to lead me not into temptation and to deliver me from evil.

July 26

The Lord bless you and keep you: The Lord make his face to shine upon you, and be gracious to you.

Numbers 6:24-25

Lord Jesus, You have been gracious to Phobics Victorious. You have shown us Your name. You have drawn us to You and revealed Your mighty power. Your light has shown on the darkness of our fear and depression.

Today, I follow the light of Jesus. He leads me on a journey out of darkness. He sets me free. In His light, I have love and peace and joy. I am still before the Lord and wait patiently for Him. He blesses me.

Fear not, for I am with you and will bless you.

Genesis 26:24

In Phobics Victorious, our Higher Power promises, that He is with us and will bless us. We receive that promise and give thanks to our God.

Thank You, dear Jesus, for blessing me. If it had not been for You, I would have perished. You have given me life. I am free in Christ. I accept abundant life, full of joy and blessings. I believe in You. I am restored to wholeness.

God is at work in you, both to will and to work for his good pleasure.

Philippians 2:13

We in Phobics Victorious know that God is good. He is love and truth. He is just. When we were in charge, our lives were a mess. With God in charge, we know that all things work for good.

I have surrendered my will and my life to the care of my Higher Power. He is at work in me. Only justice, goodness, truth, love and beauty will prevail.

May our Lord Jesus Christ...and our God our Father, who loved us and gave us eternal comfort... Comfort your hearts.
II Thessalonians 2:16-17

We in Phobics Victorious are on a pilgrimage in this world. Our eyes are set on the Kingdom of God. We follow spiritual principles.

Today, Lord Jesus, give me Your comfort as I journey through this world. Fill me with Your: peace. Lead me, guide me and walk beside me. Holy Spirit, teach me. Wrap me up in Your arms of love so that I may feel Your eternal comfort

---

Do you want to be healed? Rise, take up your pallet, and walk.
John 5:6,8

Fear paralyzes. Depression paralyzes. In Phobics Victorious, we learn new thought patterns. We learn new behavior patterns. Our minds are renewed. Our energy is renewed. This takes time.

Today, I will take the first step. I will act on my faith. I will go to a meeting. I will call a friend. I will exercise my body. I will choose life.

July 31

And Moses said unto the people, Fear not: for God is come to prove you, and that his fear may be before your faces, that ye sin not.

Exodus 20:20

To fear the Lord is a totally separate thing than to experience irrational fears and phobias. Fearing the Lord is respecting Him, and obeying His commandments; it is knowing that apart from Him there is no life.

Today, I root out sin areas in my life that keep me from the presence of God. I know when sin dwells in me. I block out God's love. Help me, Lord, not to sin today. Keep me mindful of Your presence and Your commandments.

Only rebel not ye against the Lord neither fear ye the people of the land; for they are bread for us: their defense is departed from them, and the Lord is with us: fear them not.

Numbers 14:9

In Phobics Victorious, we walk with Jesus. In His power and strength, we are protected from evil men. The Lord is our redeemer. We will fear nothing.

Today, I put on the full armor of God; righteousness, truth, the word of God, the gospel of peace, the salvation of the Lord, Jesus Christ. Through Christ, I can do all things.

August 2

Behold, the Lord thy God hath set the land before thee: go up and possess it, as the Lord God of thy fathers hath said unto thee; fear not, neither be discouraged.

Deuteronomy 1:21

Sometimes when we look around, we feel overwhelmed at the amount of evil in the land. The media seems to focus on the dark side. We can become filled with fear.

Today, I know that God is with me. My focus is on Him. I confidently walk through this day, knowing that Christ dwells in me. I possess the land.

August 3

Ye shall not fear them: for the Lord your God he shall fight for you.

Deuteronomy 3:2

In Phobics Victorious, we have God on our side. We need not fear evil. Our refuge is in our Higher Power. His Holy Spirit is more powerful than any malevolent forces.

Today, I give my cares and fears to Jesus. I do not need to carry them. He is the burden bearer. He is in the miracle working business. All I need to do is trust in Him. He will fight for me.

August 4

Therefore thou shalt keep the commandments of the Lord thy God, to walk in His ways, and to fear Him.

Deuteronomy 8:6

In Phobics Victorious we follow a spiritual journey that is outlined in the

Twelve Steps. We know that the Twelve Steps are based on the word of God. They are a direct outgrowth of Christian Biblical principles.

Help me, Lord, to keep the commandments. I am willing, but I am also often weak. In my flesh, I stumble and fall. Teach me to walk in the Spirit and to know You better.

August 5

And thy life shall hang in doubt before thee; and thou shalt fear day and night, and shalt have none assurance of thy life.
Deuteronomy 28:66

As recovering phobics, we know what it is like to suffer from doubt, confusion, and fear. These are tools of the adversary, tools that destroy us.

Today, I know I have life in Jesus Christ. He is the way, the truth, and the life. He is already victorious over the powers of darkness. He has risen from the dead and dwells with God. He has promised to return to this earth to establish His kingdom.

Be strong and of a good courage, fear not, nor be afraid of them: for the Lord thy God, he that doth go with thee: he will not fail thee, nor forsake thee.

Deuteronomy 31:6

In Phobics Victorious, we are learning to be courageous. Once our acute panic attacks and phobias are gone, we learn new, bolder behavior patterns. We become bold, yet humble; strong, yet meek.

Today I know, dear Higher Power, that You have made me a promise. I know You are with me and that You will not forsake me. You love me and have always loved me. I choose to receive the fullness of Your love.

August 7

And David said to Soloman his son, Be strong and of good courage, and the Lord God, even my God, will be with thee; he will not fail thee, nor forsake thee, until thou hast finished all the work for the service of the house of the Lord.

1 Chronicles 28:20

Sometimes we in Phobics Victorious

become weary and tired in our recovery. Usually, this happens because we have been trying too hard, carrying the load ourselves, and wanting what we want right now. But we must learn to be patient and turn our problems and desires over to God. We wait for His good in our lives.

Today, dear Higher Power, I know that in Your strength, Your power, and Your time, I will reap the rewards of Your promises — full, abundant life — free from fear, despair, and doubt.

August 8

Therefore snares are round about thee, and sudden fear troubleth thee.

Job 22:10

Many of us recovering phobics thought our panic attacks were something new. How surprised we were to find that "sudden fear" is mentioned in ancient Biblical times.

I am comforted to know that in my suffering and affliction from phobias and panic attacks, I am not alone. I have many brothers and sisters in Twelve Step fellowships in many different denominations. We are blessed to give each other our experience, strength and hope, and especially our love!

August 9

Like a father pityeth his children, so the lord pityeth them that fear Him.
Psalm 103:13

In our acute stages of panic attacks and phobias, we felt so separated from others and from the love of God. Some of our poor behaviors, because of fear, made us ashamed and guilt ridden. We thought God, the Father, would be harsh and unforgiving to us.

Today, I know that my Higher Power loves me. He understands the weakness of my flesh. He is tender and merciful full of pity and compassion. He gently lifts me and restores me to wholeness.

August 10

The fear of the Lord is the beginning of wisdom: a good understanding have all they that do His commandments.
Psalm 111:10

Our God knows what is good for His children. He created us and fashioned us in His image. His commandments are not meant to bind us, but to free us to live healthy, loving lives.

In Phobics Victorious, I look to Jesus to show me the way. In my actions and attitudes this day, I will ask myself, "What would Jesus do?" His Holy Spirit will gently guide me into truth, the truth that sets me free.

August 11

Hearken unto me, ye that know righteousness, the people in whose heart is my law; fear ye not the reproach of men, neither be ye afraid of their revilings.

Isaiah 51:7

The Twelve Steps of Phobics Victorious are a spiritual journey from darkness into light. As we become stronger in our progress, we notice that our perceptions and actions are changed.

As I go into this day, I will not be afraid at the unenlightened condition of fellow friends and acquaintances. I know who I am in Christ, a new creation, cleansed by the blood of the Lamb. He is sanctifying me, and He desires that we all become holy as He is holy.

*According to the word that I covenanted
with you when ye came out of Egypt, so my
spirit remaineth among you: fear ye not.*
                                    Haggai 2:5

God is faithful, steadfast, and just. He
keeps His promises. He is always present;
yet we, through our sinful rebellion,
separate ourselves from Him.

Today, I again surrender my life to
God the Father, to His Son Jesus Christ
and to His Holy Spirit. I choose to
relinquish self-will. I pray for His will to
be done in my life.

August 13

*Everlasting joy shall be upon your
heads: they shall obtain joy and gladness.*
                                    Isaiah 35:10

How we recovering phobics have
longed for the return of joy and gladness
into our lives. How we've missed the free,
spontaneity of youth — the childlike
simplicity of complete trust and faith.

Thank You, Lord Jesus, for giving me a
new life. I feel like a child again as I place
my trust in You. I keep it simple and seek

to love and be loved. I have come through a dark valley into the light of Your love and healing power. All life reflects Your glory and majesty.

August 14

I will restore health to you.
Jeremiah 30:17

In Phobics Victorious we are restored to health. We become new people. We lose our old negative responses, fears and unhealthy dependencies. We come to a knowledge of the living God and of His power and love in our lives.

I walk in newness of life, not feeling alone or afraid. The Lord is with me. I am filled with His Spirit. Joy, peace, and life-giving energy are being released in me. I love God, myself, and others. Thank You, Jesus, for the gift of life.

August 15

And the effect of righteousness will be peace, and the result of righteousness, quietness, and trust forever.
Isaiah 32:17

Becoming righteous is a process. Our

negative fearful natures kept us in bondage. We learned unhealthy, often sinful, behavior patterns. As we work the Twelve Steps of Phobics Victorious, we clean up our lives.

Today, I will try to be righteous. I am willing to follow Jesus. When I err, I know that I am like a child, growing spiritually. In my own flesh, I am weak. I know I often relapse into old ways of thinking and behaving. But He loves me and forgives me.

August 16

Lead me in thy truth, and teach me.
Psalm 25:5

In Phobics Victorious, we replace fear with faith. Our faith is in our Higher Power, Jesus Christ. We trust in Him, and we walk by faith. His Holy Spirit leads us into Truth; He is our Counselor, our Guide.

Fill me, Holy Spirit. Show me the way. Teach me, in love, how to choose the right path. I desire the peace, the quietness, the trust of a righteous life. I receive the love and joy of the Lord.

For I will forgive their iniquity, and I will remember their sin no more.
Jeremiah 31:34

In Phobics Victorious, we are submitted to the Lordship of Jesus Christ. Our wills are surrendered to the will of our Heavenly Father.

Today, I know that I have come home. I am a child of God, resting gently in His hands. He loves me and has forgiven and forgotten my self-willed ways. His will for me is only what is good, right and just. Thank You, Lord Jesus, for saving me.

But to which of the angels said he at any time, Sit on my right hand, until I make thine enemies thy footstool? Are they not all ministering spirits, sent forth to minister for them who shall be heirs of salvation?
Hebrews 1:13-14

In Phobics Victorious we are not alone. Our spiritual struggle against fear and doubt is aided by divine ministering spirits.

Holy Angels, place a guard around me and protect me from demon spirits. Keep me safe as I go into the world today. With the power of the Holy Spirit within and the protection of the holy angels without, I am courageous in all circumstances.

August 19

Take heed, brethren, lest there be in any of you an evil heart of unbelief, in departing from the living God.
Hebrews 3:12

The second step in Phobics Victorious says, "We came to believe that a Power greater than ourselves...". Without belief, we are unable to receive the gift of life that our God desires to give us.

Today, I will increase my belief by focusing on Jesus Christ, my Higher Power. In Him is victory over fear, disease and death. In Him is life eternal. Holy Spirit, empower me with His life and love that I might walk in total belief and faith.

For he that is entered into his rest, he also hath ceased from his own works, as God did from his. Let us labour therefore to enter into that rest, lest man fall after the same example of unbelief

Hebrews 4:10-11

We in Phobics Victorious are offered rest, peace, serenity and relief from our fears. Let us not become so busy in outlining our own recovery or in exhausting ourselves by doing too much.

Today, I rest in God. I trust in His will of good for my life. I release all negative emotions. I praise You, Lord Jesus, for Your majesty and might. You are over all in perfect goodness.

Let us therefore come boldly unto the throne of grace, that we may obtain mercy, and find grace in time of need.

Hebrews 4:16

In Phobics Victorious, we make a daily decision to come boldly to Christ. We surrender daily to Him. We know He loves us and forgives us our weaknesses.

Today, Lord Jesus, in Your tender mercy, shed more grace on us that we will be able to withstand the hardships of this life. We desire to be overcomers of fear, disease, and death. We know we already have that victory in You. We thank You and glorify Your name.

August 22

Who can have compassion on the ignorant, and on them that are out of the way; for that he himself is compassed with infirmity.

Hebrews 5:2

When one suffering phobic helps another, we offer experience, strength and hope. We offer our love and support. As we recover in Phobics Victorious, we compassionately minister to those acutely suffering.

I will remember today, that as I freely receive, I will freely give. The twelfth step tells me to carry the message. I know that a wounded healer is greatly able to help others. Let me be that healer today.

But without faith it is impossible to please Him: for he that cometh to God must believe that He is, and that He is a rewarder of them that diligently seek Him.
Hebrews 11:6

When we have come to the end of our own resources, we turn to a power greater than our selves. In Phobics Victorious, we believe in God and in His power to restore us to wholeness. We believe He loves us and desires to give us His goodness.

Today, I seek Your face, Lord Jesus. I commit my life and work, my relationships, my finances, to You. You are my Higher Power, and I can do all things through You.

August 24

If ye endure chastening, God dealeth with you as with sons; for what son is he whom the father chasteneth not?
Hebrews 12:7

Following Jesus and the Twelve Steps of Phobics Victorious is a process. It is a process of spiritual growth, salvation, and sanctification. It is not followed without

passing through some pain. Learning dis-
cipline is not easy.

Today, 0 Lord, I will remember Your
promise and Your love. I will focus on
You, knowing You see me as Your child. I
know that learning new ways to live may
be difficult now, but You will help me
through to success!

August 25

*Wherefore lift up the hands which
hang down, and the feeble knees; And
make straight paths for your feet, lest that
which is lame be turned out of the way;
but let it rather be healed.*

Hebrews 12:12-13

In Phobics Victorious, we help
each other by sharing the message of
Jesus Christ and the Twelve Steps of
Phobics Victorious. We share our own
experience, strength, and hope. Most
of all, each of us walks a spiritual path
that's narrow, but that leads to healing
and life.

Today, I pray that I may continue
in a steadfast walk with Christ. I pray
that when tired, tempted or weak, I will
remain on the path of righteousness; I
will not turn left or right.

Wherefore we receiving a kingdom which cannot be moved, let us have grace, whereby we may serve God acceptably with reverence and godly fear.

Hebrews 12:28

When we surrender our will and our life to God, we no longer live to ourselves. We live in Christ; by His grace we receive abundant life.

Today, Lord, let me remember to do lowly services of love, for I know that if I do "to the least of one of these" I do it unto You. With a thankful, reverent heart, I commit my life and service to You.

August 27

Jesus Christ the same yesterday, and today, and forever.

Hebrews 13:8

When faced with all the changes of this world — disease, divorce, and death, we often lose our bearings. Sometimes losses, whether it is a job loss, a broken relationship, or an ill loved one, accumulate one on top of another, and we lose hope.

Today, I will affirm that my Higher Power, Jesus Christ, never changes. He is the same yesterday, today, and forever; He is with me right now. Thank You, Jesus! I give You praise and glorify Your name.

August 28

By him therefore let us offer the sacrifice of praise to God continually, that is, the fruit of our lips giving thanks to his name.
Hebrews 13:15

As we recover from phobias and panic attacks, which often are accompanied by depression or substance abuse, let us look continually to our Higher Power, Jesus Christ. When others fail us, when we're at wit's end, let us keep our eyes fixed on Jesus. He is our Deliverer, our Healer, the Great Physician.

I praise You, Lord Jesus, for who You are, the Creator of Heaven and Earth. You are King of Kings, Lord of Lords. I thank You today for my recovery, and praise Your holy name.

Now the God of peace, that brought again from the dead our Lord Jesus, that great shepherd of the sheep, through the blood of the everlasting covenant, Make you perfect in every good work to do his will, working in you that which is well-pleasing in his sight, through Jesus Christ, to whom be glory for ever and ever.

Hebrews 13:20-21

In Phobics Victorious, we learn to give up our will. We turn over our life to God each day. We are no longer driving the boat, directing events. We give up control that we may gain control again of a manageable life.

Dear Lord, I know that as I submit my will to Your will this day, a perfect outworking will come in my life. I thank You, Lord Jesus. I commit this day to You.

But ye shall receive power, after that the Holy Ghost is come upon you.

Acts 1:8

We have been in bondage to a spirit of fear for so long. We phobics knew that we were not free. We could not get free on our own.

Each day, I ask my Higher Power, Jesus Christ, to give me a fresh infilling of His Holy Spirit. As I live a spirit-filled life, all of life becomes a beautiful gift. The spirit of love fills me and flows out of me. Thank You, Jesus.

August 31

And it shall come to pass, that whosoever shall call on the name of the Lord shall be saved.

Acts 2:21

In Phobics Victorious, our Higher Power is Jesus Christ. We come to Jesus, surrender our lives to Him, and ask Him to be our personal Savior. Jesus is faithful to do what He has promised. He transforms us. In Him, we are new creations.

Dear Jesus, today I come to You. I am weary and tired. My fears and depression have beaten me up. I come to rest in You and to receive a new life. I praise You, Jesus, and I love You. Hallelujah.

September 1

Thou hast made known to me the ways of life; thou shalt make me full of joy with thy countenance.

Acts 2:28

Because of phobias and acute panic attacks, we had lost our way in life. We were confined, confused, doubtful, and afraid. But we came for help. We came to Jesus, our Higher Power in Phobics Victorious. Jesus is the way.

Today, I embrace the gift of life, of love, of joy. I stop doubtful thinking. I walk by faith not fear. I know I am not alone for I have Jesus, who overcame the world. I celebrate being alive.

September 2

Then Peter said unto them, Repent, and be baptized every one of you in the name of Jesus Christ for the remission of sins, and ye shall receive the gift of the Holy Ghost.

Acts 2:38

Recovering from phobias and panic attacks, many of us realized we could not continue living and thinking the way we had. We discovered our old ways did not work. We took ourselves to the cross and gave our lives to Jesus Christ. The symbolic value of baptism lies in a total cleansing and washing away of the old self, and receiving a new life in Christ.

Thank You, Lord Jesus, for saving me and delivering me. I receive Your gift of the Holy Spirit into my life.

September 3

Then Peter said, Silver and gold have I none; but such as I have give I thee: In the name of Jesus Christ of Nazareth rise up and walk.

Acts 3:6

There is power in the name of Jesus Christ. In Phobics Victorious, we accept Jesus Christ as our Higher Power. All power and authority in and under Heaven belong to Jesus, and He offers this to us.

Today, I will offer the strength and power of Jesus to someone still suffering from phobias. I will show them how to walk in His power and strength, not their own. I know He never changes and that He is with me now. His Spirit will dwell in us. We can rest in Him.

*Repent ye therefore, and be converted,
that your sins may be blotted out.*

Acts 3:19

We who have known the bondage of
fear, phobias, panic attacks and sometimes
substance abuse or codependency, know
what it is like to repeat a certain pattern in
our lives. This is often a self-destructive
pattern. We cannot expect real change or
transformation until we acknowledge our
mistakes and turn to God.

I thank You, dear Jesus, this day, for
dying for my sins. You have already
paid my penalty. I am washed clean by
Your blood. You have lifted my burden.
Any further guilt I feel is put there only
by me. I can renounce it, for You have
redeemed me.

September 5

*Be it known unto you all, and to all the
people of Israel, that by the name of Jesus
Christ of Nazareth, whom ye crucified, whom
God raised from the dead, even by him doth
this man stand here before you whole.*

Acts 4:10

Let us in Phobics Victorious not underestimate the power of Jesus Christ, our Higher Power. It is by belief and faith that we can act in His name.

Teach me, 0 Lord, to increase my faith and belief in my everyday actions. I want to see miracles happen in my life and in others. I pray that I may glorify Your name in all the world.

September 6

Neither is there salvation in any other; for there is none other name under heaven given among men, whereby we must be saved.
Acts 4:12

We phobics had tried to find salvation in many things: physicians, medication, and therapy, but true salvation is only found in Jesus. We also come to believe and know that Jesus Christ is the Savior of this world. He saves us and delivers us. Salvation is through Jesus Christ. Every knee shall bow and every tongue shall confess that Jesus Christ is Lord.

I am not alone today in the trials and tribulations of this world. Jesus Christ, the one who overcame the world, is with me.

September 7

For the man was above forty years old, on whom this miracle of healing was shown.

Acts 4:22

Some of us in Phobics Victorious have been afflicted with phobias and panic attacks for many years. We thought there was no hope, no way out. We despaired of life itself.

Today, I give thanks for the way out: Jesus Christ. He is the way, the truth, and the life. My hope rests in Him. He delivers me from all my fears. I love Jesus and others, more and more each day.

September 8

Trust in the Lord with all thine heart; and lean not unto thine own understanding. In all thy ways acknowledge him, and he shall direct thy path.

Proverbs 3:5-6

Now that we have come to a knowledge of Jesus Christ and to a personal relationship with Him, we need to leave our burdens with Him and simply trust. Many of us in recovery will err by trying too hard. Let's keep it simple. Let's let go and let God take control.

Today, I will walk the path of faith in Phobics Victorious. I will not try to solve all my problems at once or become perfect overnight. I simply trust in Him and obey.

September 9

When thou liest down, thou shalt not be afraid: yea, thou shalt lie down, and thy sleep shall be sweet.

Proverbs 3:24

Many of us phobics had panic attacks in the night or early morning hours. We could not define these sudden fears. Let us look to our Higher Power, Jesus Christ, our Lord and Savior who has promised us sweet sleep.

Thank You, dear Lord, for loving me and for caring for me. I rest firmly in You today, knowing that in You, I am victorious. You fill me with peace.

September 10

His own iniquities shall take the wicked himself, and he shall be holden with the cords of his sins.

Proverbs 5:22

When fear takes the place of faith, belief, and hope, it becomes a soul-sickness. In Phobics Victorious, we learn not to give place to fear. We focus on Jesus Christ, our Higher Power.

Today, I will not be a servant to sin. I will quickly move away from sinful, harmful behaviors and thoughts. I will concentrate on what is good, pure, beautiful, true and peaceful.

September 11

The fear of the Lord is to hate evil: pride, and arrogance, and the evil way, and the mouth, do I hate.

Proverbs 8:13

As we follow the Twelve Steps of Phobics Victorious, we become much more spiritually enlightened. We start to see the corruption, uncleanness and ungodly areas in our lives. We become more offended by them and desire to seek that which is good and holy.

Lord, You are good and holy. I seek to be more like You today. I quickly submit to Your loving sovereignty. I praise Your name.

September 12

The fear of the wicked, it shall come upon him; but the desire of the righteous shall be granted.

Proverbs 10:24

We have a choice: to do good or to do evil. We choose to follow righteousness or wickedness. There is much fear in choosing wickedness. That is why it is so important for we recovering phobics to take our personal moral inventory on a daily basis. We cannot afford to clutter our lives with sin.

Today I will choose positive thoughts; I will speak kind words; I will offer my help to someone in pain. God will hear my prayers.

The righteous is delivered out of trouble, and the wicked cometh in his stead.

Proverbs 11:8

In Phobics Victorious, we honor our Higher Power, Jesus Christ, who delivers us from all our fears. Our hope and trust is in Him. Daily, we are conformed into His image. The choice is ours each day. Will I follow Jesus today?

I choose to follow Jesus today. I will not turn back. All material things, all financial needs, all illnesses are not important in the light of Jesus Christ. In faith, I rest in Jesus, in His love for me and His victory over the world.

September 14

The way of a fool is right in his own eyes: but he that hearkeneth unto counsel is wise.

Proverbs 12:15

Phobias and panic attacks are so powerful that we became unable to manage our own lives. The first step of recovery began when we admitted we were powerless and when we decided to seek life.

I will not try to solve my problems by myself. I will seek out godly counsel. I place my trust in God and His wisdom, mercy, and grace. I will not try to run the show anymore. Instead of directing events, I will allow events to happen.

September 15

In the fear of the Lord is strong confidence: and his children shall have a place of refuge.

Proverbs 14:26

Phobias and panic attacks often began with some traumatic situation, a fear of loss or abandonment, a moral compromise. Without God, all earthly remedies fell short of cure.

I know that I cannot manage my life or phobias without God. Masking the problem with pills or alcohol only delays recovery. I surrender myself and my phobic illness to my Higher Power, Jesus Christ. My family, too, will be blessed.

September 16

*The fear of the Lord is a fountain of life,
to depart from the snares of death.*

Proverbs 14:27

Fear of the Lord refers to respect and obedience. We are children of a Heavenly Father. He is our Creator; He knows what we need for joy and happiness. To fear God is to realize that He is sovereign and mighty and just.

I know that there is order in the universe. God sees to every detail how the planets rotate around the sun, how the cycles of day, night, and the four seasons move, how each cell in my body helps the whole. I know it is the Spirit of God that gives life and power. His Spirit is love.

September 17

Without counsel purposes are disappointed: but in the multitude of counselors they are established.

Proverbs 15:22

In Phobics Victorious, we do not solve our problems alone. We meet together with other suffering phobics to share our experience, strength, and hope. We carry the message of our Higher Power, Jesus Christ, and of the Twelve Steps to others.

Today, Lord Jesus, I commit my life, my hopes, dreams, and desires to You. I rely on Your steadfastness. You are my rock, my refuge, and I cling to You. You are right with me and will never forsake me. Thank You!

September 18

Wine is a mocker, strong drink is raging: and whosoever is deceived thereby is not wise.

Proverbs 20:1

Many people suffering from phobias and panic attacks turn to alcohol and drugs. Alcohol is a drug. When chemicals are used excessively, phobics can acquire substance abuse or chemical dependency, such as alcoholism, and drug addiction. This adds insult upon injury.

Today, I will trust in my Higher Power, Jesus Christ, to deliver me from my fears. I will not anesthetize myself with alcohol and drugs, thus blocking out an awareness of God's love and help. I will increase my belief and faith.

September 19

Boast not thyself of tomorrow; for thou knoweth not what a day may bring forth.

Proverbs 27:1

One day at a time is a phrase that is used in all Twelve Step support groups. We cannot burden ourselves with the heavy load of regrets and guilt over the past; nor can we be apprehensive about the future. We cannot afford to worry about the "What if's".

Today, I will live this day only. I will enjoy the beauty around me. I will concentrate on being kind and loving. I will be good to myself and others. If doubts or fears try to ruin my day, I will commit them to my Higher Power.

September 20

He that covereth his sins shall not prosper; but whoso confesseth and forsaketh them shall have mercy.

Proverbs 28:13

The fifth step in Phobics Victorious is admitting to God, to ourselves, and to another human being the exact nature of our wrongs. This is confession. There is a saying in recovery that we're as sick as our secrets. To become healthy, whole, and free we need to be honest.

Help me, Lord, to be honest not only with others, but with myself. Show me through the power of Your Holy Spirit where I am self-deceived. I pray today that I will not deceive, nor be deceived.

September 21

He that trusteth in his own heart is a fool: but whoso walketh wisely, he shall be delivered.

Proverbs 28:26

In Phobics Victorious, we make a daily decision to come to Christ. We surrender daily to Him. We know he loves us and forgives us our weaknesses.

Today, Lord Jesus, in Your tender mercy, shed more grace on us that we will be able to withstand the hardships of this life. We desire to be overcomers of fear, disease, and death. We know we already have that victory in You. We thank You and glorify Your name.

And his name through faith in his name hath made this man strong, whom ye see and know: yea, the faith which is by him hath given him this perfect soundness in the presence of you all.

Acts 3:16

The opposite of fear is faith. It is difficult to change a lifetime habit of fearful thinking. God did not give us the spirit of fear. In Phobics Victorious, we learn to walk by faith.

Let me gain more faith today in my Higher Power, Jesus Christ. Through His name, there is power to heal and to deliver. I accept that power in my life.

And God wrought special miracles by the hands of Paul: So that from his body were brought unto the sick handkerchiefs or aprons, and the diseases departed from them, and the evil spirits went out of them.

Acts 19:11-12

We should not underestimate the power of the Holy Spirit. When we accept Jesus Christ as our Savior, He gives us

His Spirit. It is up to us to believe and to act in faith.

Lord, help me to remember that Your Spirit which dwells in me is far more powerful than any worldly forces. Show me how to use Your gifts so that I may glorify You.

September 24

For God is not the author of confusion, but of peace, as in all churches of the saints.
1 Corinthians 14:33

When we become confused because of our phobias and panic attacks, we must remember that God is not the author of confusion. We need to focus on Him and the order in the universe and nature. God sees to every detail.

Lord, I know that discomfort comes into my life when I move away from Your presence. It is in being rebellious and defiant that I bring harm to myself. I know You never change; in You is harmony and peace.

For do I now persuade men, or God? Or do I seek to please men? For if I yet pleased men, I should not be the servant of Christ.
Galatians 1:10

In Phobics Victorious, in surrendering our lives to God and accepting Jesus Christ as our Savior, we cannot continue to put men's praise first. Most phobics, out of fear of loss, are people pleasers. Because of fear, we have compromised ourselves — who we really are — Children of God.

Today, I will keep in mind to please You first, Lord. I will submit my plans and actions to You. If anything in my behavior is disobedient to Your word, I will admit it and try to choose the right.

September 26

For brethren, ye have been called unto liberty; only use not liberty for an occasion to the flesh, but by love serve one another.
Galatians 5:13

Jesus Christ, our Higher Power, delivers us from fear. He sets us free. When we are free, we walk in liberty. The bondage of fear is broken. Suddenly we are faced with many choices of things to do, things we used to be afraid of.

Today, Lord, let me recall the gift of freedom You have given me. Let me conduct myself in a holy, right manner, always being humbly grateful for my freedom. I pray to carry out lowly services of love whenever I can.

September 27

And be not drunk with wine, wherein is excess; but be filled with the Spirit.
Ephesians 5:18

By abusing alcohol to medicate our fears, we also block out other feelings. We fill the need for the Holy Spirit with chemicals, thus delaying our spiritual growth. Abusing alcohol brings other character compromises: poor health, insanity and death.

I pray to look to Jesus today for my peace and serenity. I will not drown my fears and anxieties in alcohol. I am willing, and desire to be filled with the Holy Spirit. Come into my life, Holy Spirit.

For we wrestle not against flesh and blood, but against principalities, against powers, against the rulers of the darkness of this world, against spiritual wickedness in high places.

Ephesians 6:12

Our battle against phobias and panic attacks is not just a physical or mental one. It is also a spiritual battle; for God did not give us the spirit of fear.

I remember today that Jesus Christ has all power and authority over unclean spirits. Through the name of Jesus Christ, evil spirits or demons are cast out. There is power in the name of Jesus. In the name of Jesus Christ, I command the spirit of fear to leave my life and home. Thank You, Jesus.

September 29

That at the name of Jesus every knee should bow, of things in heaven, and things in earth, and things under the earth; And that every tongue should confess that Jesus Christ is Lord.

Philippians 2:10-11

Jesus is the way, the truth, and the life. He is King of Kings and Lord of Lords. He is the Savior of the world, the Redeemer. He restores my soul. He gives me life. Jesus died, resurrected, and ascended to Heaven. He promised to return to establish His kingdom. There will be no tears, pain, disease or death. All will dwell in love and joy.

I am not afraid of worldly problems. The victory is already won through Christ's death on the cross and His resurrection. I can do all things through Christ.

September 30

Strengthened with all might, according to his glorious power into all patience and long suffering with joyfulness; Giving thanks unto the Father, which hath made us meet to be partakers of the inheritance of the saints in light: Who hath delivered us from the power of darkness, and hath translated us into the kingdom of his dear Son.
Colossians 1:11-13

Oh, Lord Jesus, we in Phobics Victorious give You praise and honor. We glorify Your name in all the world. You have set us free from the bondage of fear. You have given us new life. Each day we walk the path of righteousness and choose to follow You. We have gone from darkness into the light.

Today, I will let my light shine before men. I will be patient, thankful, and joyful.

October 1

And let the peace of God rule in your hearts, to thee which also ye are called in one body; and be thankful.

Colossians 3:15

When we live a surrendered life in daily submission to the will of God, we experience His peace. God is sovereign. His divine plan is good. He is our Creator, and we are thankful.

I will not be in a hurry today to fix all my problems or others' problems. I will be still and allow God to guide me. I desire to stay out of God's way by not trying to force solutions.

October 2

Continue in prayer, and watch in the same with thanksgiving.

Colossians 4:2

There is power in prayer. Heavenly angelic beings are near and ready to minister help. In the eleventh step of Phobics Victorious, we use prayer to increase our conscious contact with God.

Today, I offer up prayer to my Heavenly Father. I give praise and thanks with a grateful heart. I give Him the desires of my heart. He loves me and says, "Ask and it shall be given."

October 3

Ye are all the children of light, and the children of the day: we are not of the night, nor of darkness.

1 Thessalonians 5:5

Phobias and panic attacks narrowed and confined our lives. Many sufferers became afraid to walk out into the light of day. Because of fear, many sufferers abused alcohol or drugs or got caught up in an artificial night life.

I know that the spiritual journey of the Twelve Steps is from darkness into light. This journey is a sanctification process. I pray to hold my head high this day, knowing that my behavior is holy and acceptable.

October 4

Abstain from all appearance of evil. And the very God of peace sanctify you wholly.
1 Thessalonians 5:22-23

In Phobics Victorious, the more we lead a righteous spiritual life, the more peace we have. After we are in recovery for awhile and have gained a new peace and serenity, we do not want to commit any evil or character compromise that throws us into relapse.

Lord Jesus, I commit my life to You. Sanctify me with Your Holy Spirit. Keep me from temptation, and deliver me from evil. I thank You and praise You. Amen.

October 5

Now our Lord Jesus Christ himself, and God, even our Father, which hath loved us, and hath given us everlasting consolation and good hope through grace; Comfort your hearts, and establish you in every good word and work.
II Thessalonians 2:16-17

Panic attacks cause tremendous palpitations of the heart. The fear and dread is so great, we often think we are having a heart attack. As we surrender to Jesus, we are given more and more grace. We realize we're handling situations we never could before.

Today, I am a new person in Christ. His peace dwells in me. I am growing up spiritually, just as a little baby grows up. If I am faithful, my Lord will establish me.

October 6

And the Lord shall deliver me from every evil work, and will preserve me unto his heavenly kingdom.
II Timothy 4:18

We cannot overcome all the evil in this world and in our lives by ourselves. But God can. Jesus said, "I have overcome the world." When we are submitted to Him, we have His greatness in us.

I pray, today, Lord Jesus, that You totally deliver me from fear and from evil. May my life reflect Your glory, power and grace. On my own, I can do nothing. With You, I can do all things.

For the grace of God that bringeth salvation hath appeared to all men; Teaching us that, denying ungodliness and worldly lusts, we should live soberly, righteously and godly, in this present world.

Titus 2:11-12

When we come to the end of ourselves, or the uselessness of our lives on our own, we look to God and His goodness. Pretty badly beaten up by fears and losses, we give up. The Lord meets us at our point of need.

Having come home to my Higher Power, and to myself, I desire to live a godly life. Whatever is less than pure and holy, I avoid. Help me, Lord, to do Your will and follow Your way.

October 8

Therefore he is able also to save them to the uttermost that come unto God by him, seeing he ever liveth to make inter-cession for them.

Hebrews 7:25

In Phobics Victorious, Jesus Christ is our Higher Power. Many of us have come to accept Jesus as our personal Savior. We learn that the victory is in Jesus Christ. It is His power and strength that delivers us and sets us free.

Today, I come again to my Higher Power, Jesus. I surrender my will and my life to Him. I humbly admit my inadequacy in managing my life. I'm grateful for His grace.

October 9

It is better to trust in the Lord than to put confidence in man.

Psalm 118:8

Recovering phobics have gone to many friends, relatives, counselors, and/or physicians for help. All have some helpful insights. But often, sufferers are left with the same irrational fears as before. Sometimes medicine will mask the symptoms.

Lord, in all my relations with people, and my attempts to give and receive help, let me always trust in You first. It is Your power working in all who believe, that brings transformation.

*For the enemy hath persecuted my soul;
he hath smitten my life down to the ground;
he hath made me to dwell in darkness, as
those that have been long dead.*

Psalm 143:3

Fear is a lie, a deception from the adversary. Fear is a delusion, a false belief. It distorts who we really are and makes us feel great self-condemnation. Fear is the enemy. Jesus Christ, our Higher Power, is the Savior — we are victors because of Him.

By faith in Jesus Christ, I am victorious over fear. Jesus has already defeated the enemy. I trust in Him to completely deliver me from fear and to set me free.

October 11

*I also will choose their delusions, and
will bring their fears upon them; because
when I called, none did answer; when I
spoke, they did not hear; but they did evil
before men's eyes, and chose that in which I
delighted not.*

Isaiah 66 :4

Our Heavenly Father knows what is best

for us, His children. Yet we often rebel, deviate from the truth, go our own way. Our Father requires simple childlike obedience to His will of love and good for our lives.

Today, I will humble myself before God. I come to Him and kneel before Him. He takes me in His loving arms and restores my soul.

October 12

Therefore is my spirit overwhelmed within me; my heart within me is desolate. I remember the days of old; I meditate on all thy works; I muse on the work of thy hands.

Psalm 143:4-5

Phobias and panic attacks gave us a merciless beating. Our ways of dealing with them often brought even more devastating pain. Many of us found ourselves depressed; we constantly hung on to the past and feelings of failure.

Today, in Phobics Victorious, I release all of the past. I let it go. I did what I was able to do then. I forgive others who have hurt me in the past, and I forgive myself. Today is for living abundantly. Let me love fully this day.

October 13

Hear me speedily, O Lord: my spirit faileth: hide not thy face from me, lest I be like unto them that go down into the pit.

Psalm 143:7

Sometimes the recovery process seems so difficult and painful. We often try too hard, thinking we can will ourselves to get better. We wear ourselves out. Let us remember that Jesus asks us to give Him our burdens and cares. Let's not keep taking them back.

Lord, I simply trust in You. You are faithful and just; desire only good for me. Your love never changes. You brought me out of the pit, and placed my feet upon a rock. You are my rock.

October 14

Cause me to hear thy loving kindness in the morning; for in thee do I trust: cause me to know the way wherein I should walk; for I lift my soul unto thee.

Psalm 143:8

If we are constantly in a hurry, rushing here and there; if we are trying to always map out events and timeliness; if we constantly try to change and control others, we are doomed to fail out of sheer exhaustion.

Lord, let me be still this day. I pray to feel Your love and inspiration. I wait patiently and trust in You.

October 15

Teach me to do thy will for thou art my God: thy spirit is good; lead me into the land of uprightness.

Psalm 143:10

As we grow spiritually, we are really like little children growing up all over again. But now we know that we don't know everything, and we can't run the show alone.

I humbly submit to my Higher Power, Jesus. Keep me ever mindful of Your presence. In You I take refuge.

October 16

Hear my cry, O God; attend unto my prayer. From the end of the earth will I cry unto thee, when my heart is overwhelmed: lead me to the rock that is higher than I.

Psalm 61:1-2

In Phobics Victorious, our Higher Power, Jesus Christ, is our Rock. When our feet are firmly placed on the Rock, we cannot be moved.

I rest in Jesus today. He is the same yesterday, today, and forever. Jesus has power over all earthly difficulties, even nature. He calmed the storm, walked on water, and fed the multitudes. I trust in Him.

October 17

Thou art my hiding place; thou shalt preserve me from trouble; thou shalt compass me about with songs of deliverance.
Psalm 32:7

We phobics used to hide in our homes afraid to go out to face the world. Jesus Christ is our spiritual hiding place. In Him we are delivered from fear and set free. We thank You, Lord Jesus, for hiding us under Your protection. We praise and glorify Your name.

Today, I worship almighty God, the maker of Heaven and Earth. I offer Him praises. I pray for the power of His Holy Spirit to dwell in me. In the name of Jesus, I can do all things. The Father, the Son, and the Holy Ghost are one; they offer to

dwell as one in us. I receive Your free gift
of life today.

October 18

He shall not be afraid of evil tidings:
his heart is fixed, trusting in the Lord.
Psalm 112:7

As we recover from phobias and
panic attacks, we keep our focus on Jesus
Christ. We do not expect bad news at
every turn. We are transformed. Our
minds are renewed. We are given a new
heart. Despite the changes occurring all
around us, we are fixed, trusting in God.

Lord, I look to You today to be my
Rock, my fortress. I trust in You and walk
by faith. Thank You, Jesus, for carrying
my burdens. Thank You for setting me
free. Show me by Your Holy Spirit how
to walk with You.

October 19

Unto the upright there ariseth light in
the darkness; he is gracious, and full of
compassion, and righteous.
Psalm 112:4

We thank You, Lord Jesus, for giving

us light in the darkness of our fears. We give You control of our lives for You love us and desire to give us abundant life.

Let me today reflect Jesus Christ. Let my behavior and character be righteous. Keep me compassionate of other's faults as You have compassion on mine. May Your grace abound.

October 20

But now saith the Lord that created thee, O Jacob, and he that formed thee, O Israel, Fear not: for I have redeemed thee, I have called thee by thy name; thou are mine.
Isaiah 43:1

We know that our Redeemer, Jesus Christ, lives. He is our Higher Power. He came to save us, to deliver us, to show us the way. In Him is victory over all darkness, disease, disaster and death. Through Christ, we overcome.

Thank You, Lord Jesus, for redeeming me. Your shed blood cleanses me and makes me part of God's family. Just as You rose from the dead, I, too, walk in resurrection life. Thank You, Jesus. I am Your child, a spiritual being. I receive You today.

October 21

When thou passest through the waters, I will be with thee; and through the rivers, they shall not overflow thee: when thou walkest through the fire, thou shalt not be burned; neither shall the flame kindle upon thee.

Isaiah 43:2

The words our Lord and Savior, Jesus Christ, gives us in the Holy Scriptures are promises. He asks us to come unto Him. Let us take that step today. It is by belief and faith, that we are set free.

Lord Jesus, I have faith in You and Your power over all. I trust in Your goodness and love. I desire to be with You, to follow You. I need not be afraid.

October 22

Fear not: for I am with thee: I will bring thy seed from the east, and gather thee from the west.

Isaiah 43:5

Oh, how many of us suffering phobics do not have faith in God. We become consumed by fears. Our lives become a living hell. But we know there is a way out. Jesus is that way.

Let me comprehend, Lord Jesus, Your power and majesty today. Increase my awareness of Your sovereignty and might. Show me Your unending love; be gracious unto me, a sinner.

October 23

I, even I, am the Lord; and beside me there is no savior.

Isaiah 43:11

We recognize You, Lord Jesus, as our Higher Power in Phobics Victorious. We give You honor and glory. We desire to know You more and to humble ourselves under Your mighty hand. We have tried too long to do things our own way. We've often lived godless lives.

Today, dear God, I turn my heart to You. With humility and contrition, I surrender my will and my life to You. Fill me with Your loving kindness. Keep me safe. Thank You, Jesus.

Remember ye not the former things, neither consider the things of old. Behold I will do a new thing; now it shall spring forth; shall ye not know it? I will even make a way in the wilderness, and rivers in the desert.

Isaiah 43:18-19

Recovering phobics often dwell on their past mistakes and failures. Fear left us with little self esteem or confidence. We got sick and tired of being sick and tired.

I know, today, that I am a new person in Christ. The old is put away. I let go and let God. He leads me on the path of life. Each day I am conformed more and more to His image.

I, even I, am he that blotteth out thy transgressions for mine own sake, and will not remember thy sins.

Isaiah 43:25

What a wonderful relief to know that our sins are not only forgiven, but also forgotten. We need not dwell on them anymore.

Today, I will try to be just as forgiving to others as my Higher Power is to me. I will do my best to make amends wherever necessary. I will remember that I am a minister of reconciliation, just as God, in Christ, reconciled me unto Himself.

October 26

Hear, 0 Israel, ye approach this day unto battle against your enemies; let not your hearts faint, fear not, and do not tremble, neither be ye terrified of them; For the Lord your God is he that goeth with you, to fight for you against your enemies to save you.
Deuteronomy 20:34

We are not alone in our fight over the enemy, fear. We have our Higher Power, Jesus Christ. We have the power of His Holy Spirit. We have ministering angels. Let us also utilize the power of prayer.

As I go into this day, I am not alone. Jesus is with me. My will is surrendered to Him. My life is in His hands.

*Only be thou strong and very coura-
geous, that thou mayest observe to do
according to all the law, which Moses my
servant commanded thee; turn not from
it to the right hand or to the left, that thou
mayest prosper withersoever thou goest.*

Joshua 1:7

The gift of salvation of life is free. All we
need to do is to accept it. But, as we walk
each day in newness of spirit, we choose to
obey God's holy commandments. We do
not want to jeopardize our recovery; nor
do we want to offend our Higher Power.

Today, I will walk a straight path,
holy and righteous. I will take a daily
inventory to see if I have been wrong. If
so, I will admit it.

October 28

*For I am persuaded, that neither death,
nor life, nor angels, nor principalities, nor
powers, nor things present, nor things to
come, Nor height, nor depth, nor any other
creature, shall be able to separate us from the
love of God, which is in Christ Jesus our Lord.*

Romans 8:38-39

We thank You, Lord Jesus, for Your love for us. Nothing can separate us from Your love. Your love heals us. We know perfect love hath no fear. As we follow the Twelve Steps of Phobics Victorious, we become less selfish. We learn to die to self and to live for You and others.

Today, I will contemplate on God's mighty love for me. No matter where I go, or what happens to me today, nothing can take God's love from me.

October 29

And when the men of that place had knowledge of him, they sent out into all that country round about, and brought unto him all that were diseased; And besought him that they might only touch the hem of his garment; and as many as touched were made perfectly whole.

Matthew 14:35-36

Our Higher Power, Jesus Christ, heals our disease. All we have to do is reach out to Him in faith. The rest is up to Him.

Today, I will reach out to my Higher Power. He delivers me from fear. I need not worry, for His love for me is great. He desires to give me life, peace, and joy to make me perfectly whole.

October 30

Wherefore God also hath highly exalted him, and given him a name which is above every name: That at the name of Jesus every knee should bow, of things in heaven, and things in earth, and things under the earth; And every tongue should confess that Jesus Christ is Lord, to the glory of God the Father.

Philippians 2:9-11

In Phobics Victorious, we confess that Jesus Christ is Lord. Those of us with sufficient recovery from phobias know that it is the power of Jesus that sets us free.

Today, I will be mindful of the glorious gift of God in Christ Jesus. I will focus on Him and not lose sight of His victory. I am not afraid.

October 31

Let your moderation be known unto all men. The Lord is at hand.

Philippians 4:5

Because of irrational fears, many suffering phobics acted in extreme ways and adopted compulsive behaviors. Being motivated by fear, phobics had little peace and serenity. Now we know that we need to first rest in Christ. He invites us into His rest.

When I feel anxious today or hurried and worried, I will turn to Jesus. I will avoid extreme behaviors and mannerisms. I will rest in Him. If I need to, I will pull away from the crowd and rest with Him. He gives me peace.

November 1

Those things, which ye have both learned, and received, and heard, and seen in me, do: and the God of peace shall be with you.

Philippians 4:9

The Twelve Steps of Phobics Victorious are a path to righteousness, peace, and joy. We follow this program, totally surrendered to our Higher Power, Jesus Christ.

Today, I desire to follow Jesus. I pray that my words and behavior will glorify Him. Lord, let Your light shine through my life. Let my life bring You glory and bring suffering phobics to You.

I can do all things through Christ which strengtheneth me.

Philippians 4:13

In this world, there are many frightening things to deal with: disease, economic uncertainty, violence, and death. But our Higher Power, Jesus Christ, has overcome the world. He offers us life.

Today, I choose to walk with Jesus. His power and love is above all earthly things. He is one with God the Father, and I am one with Him. I can do anything if I go in His strength. Fill me, Lord, with Your Holy Spirit. Let me walk in resurrection power.

Put on the whole armour of God, that ye may be able to stand against the wiles of the devil.

Ephesians 6:11

Recovering phobics have found that their confidence and trust is in God. We cannot look to the world for answers. The truth is in Jesus Christ. As followers of Christ, we are not conformed to the pattern of the world for much is vanity.

Today, I will consciously choose to protect myself from evil. I will read my Bible and pray. I will be righteous and true. I will obey the word of God. I will share the gospel of Jesus Christ with other suffering phobics.

November 4

Being born again, not of corruptible seed, but of incorruptible, by the word of God, which liveth and abideth for ever.
1 Peter 1:23

Phobics Victorious is a spiritual program. We find freedom from fear by a spiritual awakening. We discover that we are not only physical beings, but also spiritual beings. Our true identity is in Christ.

The Spirit of the Lord is upon me today. On my own, I can do nothing. I walk in His power and might. I am unafraid of all earthly events. His Spirit is mighty and powerful. He will work through me today.

For all flesh is as grass, and all the glory of man as the flower of grass. The grass withereth, and the flower thereof falleth away.

1 Peter 1:24

We phobics know that the physical symptoms of acute panic attacks can be devastating. We often feel totally out of control. Our heart, breathing, and muscles seem to completely malfunction. Yet, we in Phobics Victorious know we are more than physical beings. We are spiritual beings, members of Christ's family.

I will not place undue emphasis on my body's reactions. My mind is stayed on Thee. In stillness, I know that God is near. It is my spirit that is eternal through Jesus Christ.

Dearly beloved, I beseech you as strangers and pilgrims, abstain from fleshly lusts, which war against the soul.

1 Peter 2:11

Having surrendered our will and our lives to Jesus Christ, we are no longer subject to this world. We have a higher calling. By sharing the message of Jesus Christ to other suffering phobics, we are doing the work of a ministry.

Today, I pray, 0 Lord, that I will abstain from temptations to do wrong. I desire to follow a righteous path that leads to eternal life, joy, peace, and love. I pray to know the Truth that sets me free.

November 7

Who his own self bare our sins in his own body on the tree, that we, being dead to sins, should live unto righteousness; by whose stripes ye were healed.

1 Peter 2:24

Jesus is our Higher Power. He has died for us that we might live. He is more than a conqueror. We have nothing to fear.

Lord, let me not hurt You by unrighteous or unholy actions. You have already paid the price for my sins. I do not want to crucify You again. Your saving work is done at the cross. Thank You, Jesus, for saving me. Thank You for delivering me.

Finally be ye all of one mind, having compassion one of another, love as brethren, be pitiful, be courteous.

1 Peter 3:8

As recovering phobics, we've often found things didn't go exactly our way. We wanted immediate results. We tried to control and direct other people and their desires. This did not work. It only separated us from the one true power that could set us free, Jesus Christ

Just as You, Lord Jesus, had compassion on me, let me today be compassionate of others. Teach me to be merciful and forgiving. Help me to love unconditionally. I pray that I will live and let live; that I will accept what I cannot change.

November 9

For the eyes of the Lord are over the righteous, and his ears are open unto their prayers: but the face of the Lord is against them that do evil.

1 Peter 3:12

In Phobics Victorious, we learn to walk by faith, not fear. We know that as we are surrendered to God, our lives reflect His will. His will is only love and goodness for us.

Today, I pray not to depart from Your will, Lord Jesus. When I take back control of my life, let me immediately turn to You, Jesus. Let me not interfere with Your perfect outworking. I pray to be humble and submitted to You.

November 10

And above all things have fervent charity among yourselves; for charity shall cover the multitude of sins. Use hospitality one to another without grudging.

1 Peter 4:8-9

Because we have so freely received the gift of God's love and life, may we in Phobics Victorious share the message with other suffering phobics. We know it is in freely giving that we receive.

Lord Jesus, help me to remember today how You so freely gave Your life for me. Let me reflect on Your tender mercy and mighty healing power. I receive You, again, today.

November 11

Wherefore let them that suffer according to the will of God commit the keeping of their souls to him in well doing, as unto a faithful Creator.

1 Peter 4:19

There is a saying in recovery: no pain, no gain. We in Phobics Victorious know that to enter into new life, we do have to go through pain. But the new birth and life are far more glorious and joyful than we realize. If we are steadfast and endure, we know God is faithful to reward us.

Today, I will keep my eyes fixed on the high calling of Christ Jesus. He is victorious over fear, disease, evil, and death. He has promised to set me free.

November 12

The Lord also will be a refuge for the oppressed, a refuge in times of trouble.

Psalm 9:9

When all of the worldly circumstances seem despairing and gloomy, we can look to Jesus for victory. He is our rock. He will take us through the rough times. He transforms us; through our weaknesses

He makes us strong.

Today, I am submitted to Christ. He is my Redeemer. He has delivered me from fear and evil. I cast all my cares upon Him. Thank You, Jesus.

November 13

The sorrows of death compassed me, and the floods of ungodly men made me afraid.
Psalm 18:4

In Phobics Victorious, we grow into more godly people. This occurs through a sanctification process that takes place. We clean up areas of our life and no longer wish to compromise our character.

Today, I am not afraid of people, nor what they can do to me. My trust is in the Lord Jesus. His Holy Spirit dwells in me and guides me today. In knowing Jesus, the Truth, I am free.

November 14

It is God that girdeth me with strength, and maketh my way perfect.
Psalm 18:32

All our earthly endeavors did not bring complete recovery to suffering phobics.

We tried many things to conquer the fear, but, we ultimately knew that it is God who sets us free.

Today, I am strong through Jesus Christ. I will follow Him. By being surrendered to His will for me, I cannot fail. He is the way. Thank You, Jesus.

November 15

Who can understand his errors? Cleanse thou me from secret faults.

Psalm 19:12

Phobics buy into a false idea or belief about themselves. We are deluded and easily deceived. Through our spiritual program of the Twelve Steps of Phobics Victorious, we are led into the light. The light shows us the dark, self deception in ourselves.

Today, I surrender to my Higher Power, Jesus. I pray for His light to shine in my life. I desire to overcome any defects of character. I pray for the bondage of self-deception and delusion to be broken in the name of Jesus.

Turn thee unto me, and have mercy upon me; for I am desolate and afflicted. The troubles of my heart are enlarged; 0 bring me out of my distress.

Psalm 25:16 17

The major turning point in our lives as recovering phobics is when we give up. Paradoxically, it is in giving up and surrendering to our Higher Power, that we become, day by day, transformed. We need only open our minds, hearts, and life to Jesus. His Holy Spirit then does the real conversion work.

My eyes are on Jesus. I accept Him and receive His Holy Spirit. I am being renewed, transformed. I have a new life in Christ. He delivers me from evil.

0 Lord my God, I cried unto thee, and thou hast healed me.

Psalm 30:2

Many suffering phobics look everywhere for a cure, except to a Higher Power. It was only when all our manipulations and efforts to control did not work, that we fully surrendered our lives to God. What a relief to know that we no longer must carry our own cares and burdens. Jesus is our burden bearer.

Today, I believe in a Higher Power who restores me to wholeness. I increase my faith in His promises. Jesus is the Great Physician, the great healer. I receive His healing today. Thank You, Lord.

November 18

Weeping may endure for a night but joy cometh in the morning.

Psalm 30:5

It has been a long painful trail for suffering phobics. All activities and relationships were affected by fear. Additional negative coping mechanisms, such as alcohol, drugs, codependent relationships, and compulsive behaviors led to further grief. We came to our Higher Power, Jesus Christ, to renew our lives.

As I walk through the difficulties of this world, I will remember that Jesus offers me new life, full of love, peace and eternal joy. I accept His gift.

Be of good courage, and he shall strengthen your heart, all ye that hope in the Lord.

Psalm 31:24

Debilitating phobias and panic attacks made us think we would never have sufficient courage. Yet in Phobics Victorious, we have a Higher Power, Jesus Christ, who promises to give us strength.

Today, I hope in the Lord. When all else seems to be negative, I look to Jesus. He is the Alpha and the Omega, the beginning and the end. As I trust in Him and His divine plan for me, I am not afraid.

November 20

Thou art my hiding place; thou shalt preserve me from trouble; thou shalt compass me about with songs of deliverance.

Psalm 32:7

As recovering phobics in Phobics Victorious, we look to Jesus first. The Twelve Steps, which are Biblically inspired, are a program which leads to new life and freedom from fear.

Lord Jesus, in all the vicissitudes and

changes in the world, I rest in You, for You never change. You are always right with me. You protect me, keep me safe, and deliver me from evil. I seek You, Lord, today.

November 21

The Lord is nigh unto them that are of a broken heart; and saveth such as be of a contrite spirit.

Psalm 34:18

We in Phobics Victorious came to realize that we could not recover on our own. Our attempts were half-way endeavors. We often slipped back into old, unproductive ways.

Today I am aware that my Higher Power, Jesus, is with me. I may move away from Him, but He never leaves me. I hold onto You today, Lord Jesus. I commit my life to You.

November 22

My heart panteth, my strength faileth me; as for the light of mine eyes, it also is gone from me.

Psalm 38:10

On our own, we are powerless to overcome our fears. But we in Phobics Victorious have a Higher Power, Jesus Christ, who has all power and authority. We surrender our will and our lives to Jesus. In Him, we are victorious.

Today, I dwell in Christ. He has already overcome. Through Him I also overcome. O Lord, let me glorify Your name. Let Your light shine through me. Have mercy on me and give me grace.

November 23

Forsake me not, O Lord: O my God, be not far from me. Make haste to help me, O Lord my salvation.

Psalm 38:21-22

Trying to follow Jesus and to work the Twelve Steps is often difficult. The world puts pressures on us and distracts us from our true purpose. We are children of God, created in His image. He desires that we worship Him and glorify His name.

Today, I ask the Lord Jesus Christ to make Himself known to me. In His Holy name, I command all unclean forces to leave me. I pray for holy angels to protect me, my home, and family. I give thanks!

Praying always with all prayer and supplication in the Spirit, and watching thereunto with all perseverance and supplication for all saints; And for me, that utterance may be given unto me, that I may open my mouth boldly, to make known the mystery of the gospel.

Ephesians 6:18-19

Phobics Victorious is a spiritual program. In it, we learn to bring every need and concern to our Higher Power, Jesus Christ. We can pray for others, too. We are given new life. We grow spiritually and are transformed into the image of God.

Today, Higher Power, as I have prayed to help others be free of phobias, give me the right words and attitude to show what You have done in my life.

Come now and let us reason together, saith the Lord: though your sins be as scarlet, they shall be white as snow; though they be red like crimson, they shall be as wool.

Isaiah 1:18

We are not alone in Phobics Victorious. What a relief to find out that we are forgiven for the sins we have committed. Guilt has no place in our life anymore. All we have to do is give our life over to Christ. He offers us a free gift — eternal life.

Jesus, I know You have already paid the price for my sins. I am cleansed through the blood of the Lamb. I thank You, Jesus, for saving me. Thank You for Your comfort and peace.

November 26

Woe unto them that are wise in their own eyes, and prudent in their own sight.
Isaiah 5:21

All of our worldly knowledge could not free us from our irrational fears, phobias, and panic attacks. We needed a power greater than ourselves. That power is the Lord Jesus Christ. Without Jesus, we can do nothing. With Jesus, we can do all things.

I pray that I will not get in Your way, O Lord. I cast all my cares on You. I let go and let God this day. I can't, but You can! Thank You, Jesus.

For unto us a child is born, unto us a son is given; and the government shall be upon his shoulder: and his name shall be called Wonderful, Counselor, The mighty God, The everlasting Father, The Prince of Peace.
Isaiah 9:6

In Phobics Victorious we have a mighty Counselor, the great Physician, and the great Healer. By faith in His name, we are healed.

Thank You, Jesus, for delivering me from fear. I praise Your name. Thank You for setting me free. Fill me with Your Holy Spirit that I might live in resurrection power.

Therefore the Lord himself shall give you a sign, Behold, a virgin shall conceive, and bear a son and shall call his name Immanuel.
Isaiah 7:14

Our Higher Power is Jesus Christ. He came as a tiny babe in a humble home, to a young virgin named Mary. That was God's sign to us — But He is King of Kings, and Lord of Lords. He is the

Alpha and the Omega, the Great I Am. He is the Savior, the Messiah. He has overcome the world.

Today, I will follow Jesus. I will not turn back. He restores my soul. He redeems me. He brings me out of the pit and places my feet on a rock. He renews me. He gives me new life.

November 29

The people that walked in darkness have seen a great light: they that dwell in the land of the shadow of death, upon them hath the light shined.

Isaiah 9:2

In the darkness of our phobias and fears, You, Lord Jesus, our Higher Power, have shone a light. We follow that light. One day at a time, we journey from darkness to light. Let Your light shine in and through us.

Fill me, Jesus, with Your Holy Spirit. Any areas of darkness in my life, I command, in the name of Jesus, to depart. I pray to let my light shine and to glorify God.

November 30

I have said ye are gods; And all of you are children of the most High.

Psalm 82:6

As spiritual beings and as Children of God, we have a divine inheritance. The Creator dwells in us, and we can do all things. Without our Creator, we are powerless.

Through Jesus Christ, I can do all things. I am a member of the family of God. I need not be afraid. I am a saint in God's eyes; holy angels hover round me. There is victory in the name of Jesus.

December 1

Fill their faces with shame; that they may seek thy name, 0 Lord.

Psalm 83:16

Phobias and panic attacks brought a lot of shame on us. Compulsive behavior patterns, and substance abuse, added even more shame. Only a power greater than ourselves could save us. That power is Jesus Christ.

I come to You today, Lord Jesus. I bring my shame, my mistakes, my pain and despair to You. I place them at the foot of the cross. Your blood cleanses me from all sin. I am free. Thank You, Jesus.

December 2

Thou hast set our iniquities before thee, our secret sins in the light of thy countenance.
Psalm 90:8

Bringing our fears and our sins into the light of our Lord and Savior, Jesus Christ, can be very painful. Sin is not pretty, and when it is exposed it is hideous. Having seen and confessed our sins, our Higher Power, Jesus, forgives us and cleanses us.

I pray today to see myself clearly. I do not want to deceive myself. Any sin that would separate me from the love of God, I confess and give up. All I need is God's love in my life.

December 3

Thou shalt not be afraid for the terror by night; nor for the arrow that flieth by day.
Psalm 91:5

We phobics have been fearful of many things. Our Higher Power, Jesus, tells us recovering phobics to not be afraid. In fact, He tells us this many, many times. Through faith in Jesus Christ, we are set free from our fears. Our hope and trust is in Him.

My creator and Lord is faithful and true and just. He loves me with an everlasting love. He desires to dwell with me and to give me His Spirit. He gives me grace and strength and courage. I will trust, and not be afraid.

December 4

Because thou hast made the Lord, which is my refuge, even the most High, thy habitation, There shall no evil befall thee, neither shall any plague come nigh thy dwelling.

Psalm 91:9-10

In Phobics Victorious, we have the spiritual presence of our Higher Power, Jesus Christ, and His holy angels. Jesus is our Savior and Deliverer.

Today, I seek You, Lord Jesus, with all my heart. I cannot withstand the powers of darkness of fear on my own. Please send Your Holy Spirit to guide me and send holy angels to protect me and my home.

He shall call upon me, and I will answer him. I will be with him in trouble; I will deliver him and honour him.

Psalm 91:15

We are so grateful to our Higher Power, Jesus Christ. He has promised to be with us in our troubles and to deliver us. We praise Your name, Lord Jesus. We submit our lives into Your care. You are our Shepherd, and we are Your sheep.

I come unto You, Lord Jesus. I bring You my fears and my cares. I cast my burdens upon You, for You care so much for me.

December 6

When my soul fainted within me, I remembered the Lord; and my prayer came in unto thee, into thine holy temple.

Jonah 2:7

It is often too easy to get caught up in the cares and anxieties of this world. We worry about finances, relationships, diseases, crime. But we, in Phobics Victorious, shift our focus to Jesus Christ. He is more than a conqueror. Our faith and trust is in Him.

Today, I will live simply, putting my trust in God. I will try to obey Him and live a righteous life. Let my actions and words reflect Your love, O Lord. Lead me on the path of life.

December 7

The Lord is good, a stronghold in the day of trouble, and he knoweth them that trust in Him.

Naham 1:7

When all else failed, we suffering phobics turned to a power greater than ourselves. It was when we totally surrendered to our Higher Power, Jesus Christ, that we reached the turning point. We were no longer alone. We had sought out our Heavenly Creator, and He was right there with us. He is a stronghold for us.

O Lord, let me remember this day that You are my protector. Goodness, love, beauty, joy, peace, truth, glory, power is who You are. You are not far from me, but with me at all times. Teach me to rest in You and receive Your life.

And God shall wipe away all tears from their eyes, and there shall be no more death, neither sorrow, nor crying, neither shall there be any more pain for the former things are passed away.

Revelation 21:4

We phobics found that doing things our way, turning away from God, only led to despair and destruction. We shed many tears. Our real recovery came with seeking our Higher Power and having a spiritual awakening. With a spiritual awakening, we no longer lived just to self. The bondage of self was broken, and we looked outward not inward.

Today, I know that God is good and true. He is faithful to us as our Creator. He has promised to wipe away all tears and pain. I trust in Him.

December 9

He that overcometh shall inherit all things; and I will be his God, and he shall be my son.

Revelation 21:7

Like little children who are disobedient,

we recovering phobics often disobeyed the precepts of our divine Creator. We, like sheep, went astray. The enticements and false fears of the world drew us apart from the refuge of God. Yet we realized we were not only unhappy, we were also very lost.

Today, I turn to Jesus Christ, my Higher Power. Through Jesus, I am redeemed and saved. He overcame the sins of the world. In, by, and through Jesus Christ, I am an overcomer. I commit myself daily to Jesus and receive His free gift of life.

December 10

But the fearful and unbelieving, and the abominable and murderers, and whoremongers and sorcerers, and idolaters, and all liars, shall have their part in the lake which burneth with fire and brim stone, which is the second death.

Revelation 21:8

When fear becomes a way of life and blots out all hope and faith and trust, it is a sin. Our Lord has told us to not be afraid, but to believe and have faith. Phobias became delusions, false beliefs. The spirit of fear is not from God.

Today, I increase my belief. I resist fearful thoughts, and I turn to Jesus. I choose to walk by faith. I believe in Jesus. I believe He dwells in me. I have faith that I can do all things through Christ.

December 11

And, behold, a woman which was diseased with an issue of blood twelve years, came behind him and touched the hem of his garment. For she said within herself, If I may but touch his garment, I shall be whole.
Matthew 9:20-21

When we come to Christ, our Higher Power in Phobics Victorious, we know that just being in His presence brings us miraculous, powerful, healing, virtue and energy. Yet many suffering phobics have trouble believing in a Higher Power. Many do not want to admit defeat or to surrender their lives. Yet we know that healing, deliverance and freedom are right there, if we but reach out

I come to You today, Lord Jesus. I touch Your hem. Your Holy Spirit fills me with healing energy, and I am not afraid.

He that findeth his life shall lose it, and he that loseth his life for my sake, shall find it.

Matthew 10:39

As recovering phobics, we realize that we have been given the gift of life, of freedom from our fears. We need to share this gift with others. God's flow of healing energy and love and power needs to continuously move through us to others. We become lights in darkness. We radiate our newfound freedom, strength and courage.

Higher Power, Jesus Christ, I no longer live unto myself. I seek to do Your will. I pray that I will reflect Your goodness, love and power. I pray to think of others more than myself, to love unconditionally, to be merciful, kind and compassionate.

For this people's heart is waxed gross. And their ears are dull of hearing, and their eyes they have closed, lest at any time they should see with their eyes, and hear with their ears, and should understand with their heart, and should be converted and I should heal them.

Matthew 13:15

Following the Twelve Steps of Phobics Victorious is a conversion experience. It is a spiritual journey to freedom. True, complete healing is from our Higher Power. In humbling ourselves before Him, we are able to receive His love and grace. When we try to run the show, to direct, control, and manipulate, we stand in God's way.

Today, I humbly ask my Higher Power to remove my shortcomings. Thank You, Jesus. May I reflect Your glory.

December 14

Whosoever therefore shall humble himself as the little child, the same is greatest in the Kingdom of Heaven.

Matthew 18:4

Little children often have more faith and trust than adults. Suffering phobics found fearful results when they put their trust in people, money, alcohol or worldly quests for power and prestige. All these objects of pursuit could be lost, leaving us lonely and abandoned. But when we humbled ourselves before God and put our trust in Him, we became settled, strengthened and established.

Lord, I trust in You and the power of Your might. I see You in others and know that Your divine plan is at work. I am firmly implanted in Your love and know that all things work together for good to those who love You.

December 15

For if a man thinketh himself to be something, when he is nothing, he deceiveth himself.

Galatians 6:3

Suffering phobics took a terrific battering until they came to a point of admitting their fears and desiring help. Many thought they could recover through their own resources. Many simply avoided the problem or escaped reality through chemicals. Tired of living bound by fear and panic, we came to Phobics Victorious for help. There we found not only help, but also a new life in Christ, healthy, whole and free.

Thank You, Lord Jesus, for revealing Yourself to me. I give You praise and want my personal relationship with You to deepen. I know that You are my Savior and Deliverer. It is only through You that I am free.

December 16

Whereas ye know not what shall be on the morrow; For what is your life? It is even a vapour that appeareth for a little time and then vanisheth away.

James 4:14

Suffering phobics get bound in negative fearful thinking habits. These thought patterns become engrained like tapes that play over and over again. Constant worry and regret over the past and anxious apprehension over the future, rob us of the beauty and joy of today. We have no guarantees of tomorrow, and the past is past. Let us live today only.

Lord Jesus, the only moment of time is now. I desire to live this moment unto

You. Show me Your life and love and grace. Let Your glory be reflected in all I see and do. I desire Your beauty, truth and peace today.

December 17

Is any among you afflicted? Let him pray.
James 5:13

The eleventh step in Phobics Victorious is to seek through prayer and meditation to improve our conscious contact with God. Many of us suffering phobics, so bound by fear and anxiety, or often not sober-minded enough to think clearly, did not utilize the power of prayer. Slowly, we learned that there is power in prayer. Prayer mobilizes holy angels to our defense. Prayer unleashes the power of Almighty God in our lives.

0 Lord, I know You desire that I worship You in Spirit and truth. Praying in the Spirit intercedes where I cannot. I desire to pray in the Spirit and receive this gift today.

December 18

And the prayer of faith shall save the sick, and the Lord shall raise him up, and if he have committed sins, they shall be forgiven him.

James 5:15

We thank You so very much, Lord Jesus, that You have drawn us to Yourself. We thank You for Phobics Victorious and a program to lead us to You. We have been deceived by fear too long, and now we are eternally grateful to walk by faith.

Today, by faith in the name of Jesus Christ, I am free from all fear. Through Christ, I am an overcomer. The victory is already won.

December 19

For the Lord searcheth all hearts and understandeth all the imaginations of the thoughts; if thou seek him, he will be found of thee.

1 Chronicles 28:9

What a wonderful blessing to know that we in Phobics Victorious are not alone. When we come to the fellowship for help, we not only find comfort in other recovering phobics, but we also find life itself, in our Higher Power, Jesus Christ.

I thank You today, Lord Jesus, for hearing my prayers. I am grateful for Your love and grace and for giving me a new life in You. Teach me to walk with You and to do Your will.

December 20

Thine, 0 Lord, is the greatness, and the power, and the glory, and the victory, and the majesty: for all that is in the heavens and in the earth is thine; thine is the kingdom, 0 Lord, and thou art exalted as head above all.

1 Chronicles 29:11

Our Higher Power, Jesus Christ, is a mighty God. He is King of Kings and Lord of Lords. We exalt His holy name. In Phobics Victorious, He gives us Himself. He gives us new life full of resurrection power. He sets us free.

This day I praise Your name Lord Jesus. You have set me free from the bondage of fear, disease and death. I am filled with Your spirit and Your love.

For the thing which I greatly feared is come upon me, and that which I was afraid of is come unto me.

Job 3:25

Many suffering phobics found that they actually brought about the things they feared the most. It was almost as if fear was a destructive form of energy that materialized. In Phobics Victorious, we realized that fear is a false belief, a lie, a delusion. We walk by faith in our Higher Power, Jesus Christ. When attacks of fear come, we focus on Jesus and His overcoming power.

I have victory over fear in Jesus Christ. He is all I need. He has given me His life, and I commit my life to Him. Through faith in Jesus, repentance, forgiveness of sin, through baptism and the infilling of the Holy Spirit, we overcome the world.

When I lie down, I say, "When shall I arise, and the night be gone? And I am full of tossings to and fro unto the dawning of the day.

Job 7:4

Many suffering phobics have panic attacks in the night. Sudden nocturnal awakening for no apparent reason leave sufferers confused and shaken. As we recover in Phobics Victorious, our Higher Power, Jesus, gives us rest. He gives us His peace that passeth all understanding.

This day I reflect on the peace of our Lord Jesus Christ. I am still and quiet; I wait patiently for Him. He is faithful to fulfill His promises, and to give me rest. I humble myself before God and trust in Him.

December 23

My soul is weary of my life; I will leave my complaint upon myself; I will speak in the bitterness of my soul.

Job 10:1

Many suffering phobics reach a low point in their lives or a bottom in which they despair even of life itself. It is at this low point that we turn to a power greater than ourselves. Realizing that left to our own devices, we are unable to solve our problems, we come to God. We humbly surrender our wills and life to Him.

Today, I know that in Christ all things are new. I am no longer in bondage to self, but through surrender to Jesus and through baptism, I died to self. Today, I walk in newness of life, full of grace, and love and truth.

December 24

If iniquity be in thine hand, put it far away, and let not wickedness dwell in thy tabernacles. For then shalt thou lift up thy face without spot; yea, thou shalt be steadfast, and shalt not fear.

Job 11:14-15

In following Jesus and the Twelve Steps of Phobics Victorious, we cleaned up our lives. Our spiritual growth is a gradual process. We realized that we are to be holy as God is holy. Having received forgiveness for shortcomings and freedom from fears, we did not want to hurt our newfound peace and serenity in any way. Anything that would separate us from God had to go.

I know this day that as I walk righteously with the Lord, I can hold my head up high. I can look at others in the eye and be confident. God loves me and dwells in me.

December 25

For I am the Lord your God: ye shall therefore sanctify yourselves, and ye shall be holy; for I am holy.

Leviticus 11:44

Our God has told us to sanctify ourselves. We are to become pure. Let us in Phobics Victorious take the fourth step, a personal and fearless moral inventory of ourselves. Let us pray that all deception, including self-deception, be brought to light. We know that there is forgiveness for sin through our Savior, Jesus Christ. His blood cleanses us from all sin.

Thank You, Lord Jesus, for taking all my sins and nailing them to the cross. You have already paid the price and redeemed me. I need not feel any guilt. I forgive myself as You have already forgiven me. May I be merciful and forgiving to others this day.

If ye walk in my statutes, and keep my commandments, and do them; I will give peace in the land, and ye shall lie down, and none shall make you afraid.

Leviticus 26:3,6

Our Heavenly Father, our Creator, knows what is good for us in order to live joyous, abundant lives. He sent His Son, Jesus Christ, to show us the way. Just as God the Father, His Son Jesus Christ and His Holy Spirit are one, we can also be one with them. As we receive Jesus Christ as Lord and Savior, He gives us His Spirit. We are members of a heavenly family. Each day we choose to obey His commandments.

Today, I choose to do the will of my Higher Power, Jesus Christ. He intercedes for me to my Heavenly Father and confesses me before Him. I receive the love of God into my heart, and I am not afraid.

When Jesus heard it, he saith unto them, They that are whole have no need of the physician, but they that are sick: I came not to call the righteous, but sinners to repentance.

Mark 2:17

Many suffering phobics found in recovery that they had somehow transgressed some of the holy precepts of God. Through some immoral act or dishonest deed, suffering phobics seemed to experience greater fears. Idolatry is putting anything ahead of God — a person, money, fame, or power. When we put trust and faith in idols, we are insecure and anxious, for we can always lose them; But our Higher Power, Jesus Christ, is the same forever. He is the Great I Am.

I know this day, Lord Jesus, that You came to save me, to heal me, and give me new life. I accept You today, and I give You praise and glory and thanks.

But he turned, and said unto Peter, Get thee behind me, Satan: thou art an offense unto me: for thou savourest not the things that be of God, but those that be of men.

Matthew 16:23

When we in Phobics Victorious have a spiritual awakening, we find that we no longer live to please men or the world, but to please God. We try to keep ourselves away from the evil of this world. We take a daily moral inventory of ourselves. When we're wrong, we promptly admit it.

I pray this day that I will walk in faith and in peace with all men. I will choose to fulfill the greatest commandment of all: to love one another. I ask that all bitterness and resentment over wrongs committed to me, be dissolved in the light and love of God.

December 29

Whosoever therefore shall confess me before men, him will I confess also before my Father which is in heaven.

Matthew 10:32

In Phobics Victorious, we confess Jesus Christ as our Higher Power. He is our Savior and Lord. Jesus came that we might have abundant life. He is the Great Healer, Deliverer. He has overcome the world. He died and rose from the dead. He ascended into Heaven and will return one day. As believers, we are in the Kingdom of God, divine inheritors of our Creator.

I pray this day to be filled with the Holy Spirit of God. May I reflect Christ's power and glory and spread the Good News to others who still suffer without Him. May His light and love dispel all areas of darkness. Give me the joy of salvation.

December 30

Then saith Jesus unto him, Get thee hence, Satan: for It is written, Thou shall worship the Lord thy God, and him only shalt thou serve.

Matthew 4:10

As we walk a spiritual path in Phobics Victorious, and continue to sanctify our lives by the power of God's spirit, we will face many trials and temptations. But we need not fear, for we have the greatest power in the universe dwelling in us. Through the name of Jesus, we are conquerors and victors.

Today, I walk with Jesus. There is power in His name. He creates in me a clean heart. He restores my soul. He redeems me and transforms my life. I live not by my own strength, but by His.

December 31

Heaven and earth shall pass away: but my words shall not pass away.
Matthew 24:35

As we choose to develop spiritually, we recovering phobics in Phobics Victorious, follow the spiritual path of the Twelve Steps. We also find that we need to meditate on the Word of God as found in the Holy Bible. Our Lord's spirit brings light on His words, and we are continually given greater wisdom and insight.

Lord, let me reflect upon Your words today in the Holy Scriptures. May they be a light unto my path. I choose to obey Your words, Jesus, and to live the abundant, joyous, free life that You offer to me. May Your Love fill me completely and spread to others.

How to Conduct a
Phobics Victorious Meeting!

In Phobics Victorious support group meetings we concentrate on the Twelve Steps of Phobics Victorious, on the Holy Scriptures, on our meditation text, One Day at a Time in Phobics Victorious, and first and foremost, we focus on Jesus!

For suffering phobics wishing to fellowship with each other in Phobics Victorious support group meetings, the following information is helpful.

As there are no leaders, just trusted servants, the trusted servant initiating a Phobics Victorious meeting should pick a location, a time of day, 1 to 2 hours once a week, and should place information in a local newspaper, on fliers, etc.

The group facilitator gains trust by acknowledging that all information shared at meetings is strictly confidential. People meet to share their experience, strength and hope.

The format is flexible. One of the Twelve Steps can be studied, or a page, or pages, from the One Day at a Time in Phobics Victorious can be discussed.

Each meeting can be opened with

a short, simple prayer. The facilitator introduces himself and each participant shares his/ her first name only. The Twelve Steps are read. The introduction in One Day at a Time in Phobics Victorious is read. The facilitator tells a little bit about his past experiences with the disorder, his phobias or his panic attacks.

The group then discusses the topic: a step, a meditation, or a subject out of the program, such as powerlessness, belief, surrender or general sharing. One is free to share or not.

Sharing is always on a voluntary basis. Sharing does not have to go around in a circle. Circle sharing can be especially stressful to phobics. At the close of the meeting, participants join together in the closing prayer of choice, usually the Lord's Prayer.

A basket is passed for a voluntary donation, usually a dollar, to help cover housing and refreshment costs.

Information regarding Phobics Victorious meeting location and times should be sent to rosemaryjane@dc.rr.com. This information will be available to all seeking help.

Individual Phobics Victorious groups

can prepare phone lists for the participants, so members can seek assistance or keep in touch between meetings.

Phobics Victorious is here to proclaim the name of Jesus as Lord and Savior and Higher Power. Phobics Victorious is here to offer love and hope in the Spirit of our fellowship.

We invite you to come to Jesus, to learn of Him. We invite you to fellowship with other recovering phobics in Phobics Victorious meetings. Start a meeting. It only takes two. We pray that God's grace will rest on you and that His Holy Spirit will guide you into Truth and Freedom.